THE PLANETS

THE PLANETS

Sasha Fenton

Aquarian/Thorsons
An Imprint of HarperCollins*Publishers*

The Aquarian Press
An Imprint of HarperCollins*Publishers*
77–85 Fulham Palace Road
Hammersmith, London W6 8JB
1160 Battery Street
San Francisco, California 93111 – 1213

Published by The Aquarian Press 1994
10 9 8 7 6 5 4 3 2 1
1 3 5 7 9 10 8 6 4 2

A catalogue record for this book
is available from the British Library

ISBN 1 85538 352 7

Phototypeset by Harper Phototypesetters Limited,
Northampton, England
Printed in Great Britain by HarperCollinsManufacturing Glasgow

Contents

I dedicate this book to my friend, Denise
Stuart, who has now discovered the joy and
the pain of being a professional astrologer. It
was Denise who bump-started me on my way
with this book over more than a couple of
drinks on a patio in Florida.

Acknowledgements

I acknowledge my family because I know that this is the first bit of the book that they will look at! Thanks to Tony, Helen and Stuart for always having faith in me and for acting as sales team, chauffeurs, computer mending service and public relations agency. Stuart is now a writer himself, among other things, and I thank him for allowing me to pinch some of his pithier phrases. Spock would approve!

To Frank Anderson for being patient enough to nit-pick his way through the proofs of yet another book.

To Jonathan Dee who cheered himself up during a difficult phase by supplying me with some of the deeper and more fascinating pieces of information in this book. You won't have time to drift and dream any more now, Jon!

To Nina Ashby for useful information on the elements and qualities.

To David Brawn for supplying the 'astrological body'!

To Jeanette Gurney for word-processing, spotting errors and putting up with me.

To everyone else who has so generously supplied me with ideas over the years.

The snatches of song which introduce each planet come from various Gilbert and Sullivan operettas. This information was supplied by Jonathan Dee.

Introduction

I wrote the final notes to this book in the Writer's Bar in the Raffles Hotel in Singapore. Signed photographs of Somerset Maugham, Rudyard Kipling and Joseph Conrad stood on a shelf behind and to the right of me. I hope the inspiration that I gained from being in such a place and among the spirits of such noteworthy company (in addition to the Bourbon highball that was on the table in front of me), has helped to produce something really useful to aspiring astrologers. It is interesting to find that, as I was completing the notes in that exotic setting, my progressed Moon was reaching the very end of my sixth house, and that all this was going on in the sign of Sagittarius. How appropriate for the completion of such a project in such a far flung place.

This book looks into astrological effects of the planets in the Solar system in depth, and shows how their energies work through the various signs and houses. As usual, I have tried to make things simple for the beginner while, at the same time, making them interesting to the skilled astrologer. I learned a lot while writing this book, mainly by trawling through my own mind for descriptions and explanations of planetary behaviour, as well as talking to other tried and trusted astrologers. I am sure that I could find much more to say about this subject both now and in the future, because astrology is such a large and many-faceted subject that one never stops accumulating knowledge. Use the information in this book as a springboard for your own studies and learn, as I did, by looking at birthcharts and talking to the people they represent. This book only covers natal charting; predictive astrology would require a couple of books in its own right.

CHAPTER 1
Basic Information

In this book, I frequently use the terms 'he' and 'him' to indicate either sex but, where appropriate, I use he/she or even he or she.

The word 'horoscope' means a map of the hour or, in other words, a map of the sky at the moment that anything comes into existence. This could be the birth of a person, the beginning of an enterprise, a political party or, indeed, any event which has a definite beginning.

Some Helpful Information
For Beginners And Others

If you are very new to astrology, you will become fascinated when you find out where the planets were when you were born and what they reveal about your character. You will soon want to know about your ascendant (or rising sign) and the astrological houses which work their way around the horoscope from the ascendant degree. However, for the time being, simply concentrate on finding planetary positions for yourself, your family and your friends and seeing what they mean.

There are various ways in which you can find the planetary positions. If you are only ever likely to want to understand your *own* horoscope, you could send off to one of the many firms which offer computerised or hand-produced astrological readings, because these usually supply a list of the planetary positions near the front of their printouts. If you want to look at more than one chart, you will need to buy an 'ephemeris', or book of astrological tables. You can get these from any shop which specialises in New Age books or any bookshop which has a good astrology section. Alternatively, you can order one of these from one of the mail order firms which advertise in astrology magazines.

If you do decide to invest in an ephemeris, it is worth getting one which has the tables set out for *midnight* on each day rather than for *noon*. If you are only going to look up the planetary positions, it doesn't really matter which type of ephemeris you buy, but if you are likely to want to progress to full chart erection, then using a midnight ephemeris means that you won't have to calculate *backwards* for births which took place before noon. My own favourite ephemeris is called the 'World Ephemeris for the 20th Century 1900 to 2000 at Midnight'. It is published by Para Research of Gloucester, Massachusetts.

If you decide that you do want to learn how to calculate the ascendant and houses, you can find the information you need in my book, *Understanding Astrology*. Another of my books, *Rising Signs* also shows you how to calculate ascendants and house systems. There are many astrology courses available, whether you choose to study by post or by attending classes, and more books than you could ever wish to buy, so you shouldn't have any trouble finding the information you want!

There are many computer programs now available which take all the work out of chart calculation. The people who supply these are aware that a student astrologer is unlikely to have the latest state of the art equipment, so there are still plenty of programs around which will work on battered old computers. If you are becoming even slightly serious about astrology, equip yourself with a basic program which will give you a natal chart with two or three house systems, a progressed horoscope and perhaps the ability to fit one chart around another for the purposes of comparison. Your local astrology magazine will have advertisements from all the astrology computer companies and these will be happy to send you a brochure showing the kind of programs they supply.

————————**Worldwide Information**————————

Whatever level of astrology you are at, and wherever you live in the world, you would benefit by obtaining a copy of the astrology journal which is put out free of charge by the Urania Trust. Their address is as follows: The Urania Trust, 396 Caledonian Road, London N1 1DN (Tel: 071-700-0639). The current year's booklet is called *Astrology 1994: The Free Guide to Astrology in Europe and the UK*. Despite its Europe and UK title, this gives a good deal of worldwide information on publications, conferences, computer equipment and everything else to do with astrology. You may have to do some further research to pin down sales outlets in your own neighbourhood, but the addresses in this booklet will give you an excellent starting point.

Send an A5 (medium large) envelope with your name and address on it and enough money to cover postage back to you. Don't send stamps or coins in your local currency; send a postal or money order, an international reply coupon, or even two or three US dollars to cover the cost.

CHAPTER 2

Astronomical Data

Astrologers deal with the planets of the Solar system, and also the Sun and the Moon and the groups of distant stars which pass overhead, along the ecliptic. (The ecliptic is the apparent path of the Sun, Moon, planets, etc. when one looks up at the sky.) People from the distant past considered that the pattern and shape of the fixed or distant stars looked like animals or people and objects from their daily lives, and it was they who gave the signs of the zodiac their names. Some astrologers also use the larger asteroids, the nodes of the Moon and the 'part of fortune'. It all depends upon which computer program they are using at the time.

The Solar system

The Solar system comprises nine planets, including the Earth and a belt of asteroids, all of which orbit a minor yellow dwarf star which we call the Sun. Our Sun is located at the edge of a galaxy and, while there are many other stars (or Suns) in this galaxy, at the time of writing, none have been found to have planetary systems around them. This doesn't mean that there *are* no other planets or that life does not exist in some form on some distant galaxy. One group of stars in our own galaxy which seems to be in the early stages of planetary formation is called T Tauri.

The Solar system came into existence around 4,500 million years ago. The planets in our system were formed of gas and dust which was caught by the Sun's gravity. Opinions differ as to whether this material had originally been part of the Sun itself or whether it was captured in passing, so to speak. Perhaps the answer is a bit of both. The orbits of Mercury, Venus, Earth and Mars are almost circular but the outer planets' orbits are elliptical. All the planets, except Mercury and Pluto, orbit the Sun on the plane of the ecliptic.

The term 'plane of the ecliptic' is the path that the Sun *appears to take* on its journey round the Earth. The Sun, as we all know, does not travel round the Earth but, if you watch it out of your window from time to time, and if you also watch the path of the Moon and the stars, you will soon see what the early astronomers saw, i.e. the Sun, Moon, stars and planets *appearing* to travel around the Earth.

————————The Sun————————

The Sun's mean distance from Earth is 149,597,870 kilometres, and it is 333,400 times larger than the Earth. It takes 26.9 Earth days to rotate on its axis and its mean surface temperature is 5,700 kilowatts. It emits electromagnetic radiation of various wavelengths, some of which are harmful to life. Most of these used to be absorbed by the Earth's atmosphere, but that is no longer the case, due to the depletion of the ozone layer. The radiation of heat and light from the Sun makes life possible on Earth but, unless we do something *soon* about preserving the ozone layer, it may begin to make life on Earth as impossible as it now is on Venus.

————————The Planets————————

Moving outwards from the Sun, the planets are in the following order. The first is Mercury, then Venus, Earth, Mars, the asteroid belt, Jupiter, Saturn, Uranus, Neptune and Pluto. There are times, however, when Pluto actually travels inside the orbit of Neptune. In terms of size, Pluto is the smallest planet, followed by Mercury, Mars, Venus, Earth, Neptune, Uranus, Saturn and Jupiter.

Mercury, Venus, Earth and Mars are all rocky and therefore called 'terrestrial' planets. Mercury is the closest to the Sun, being within its corona, it is also the second smallest planet and its surface temperature is very high. Its surface is very similar to that of the Moon. Being small, it has little gravity and, therefore, little atmosphere. What little there is mainly comprises hydrogen and helium. Venus is covered by dense clouds which comprise carbon dioxide and sulphuric acid. The surface of the Earth is mainly covered by water and partially covered by cloud and it has one satellite which is, of course, the Moon. Earth's atmosphere comprises oxygen, carbon dioxide, nitrogen and water vapour. Mars is mainly rocky desert with polar ice caps. These ice caps were once liquid seas because there is plenty of evidence of water erosion on Mars. Mars also has active volcanoes but little atmosphere. What there is comprises carbon dioxide, oxygen and water vapour. Mars has two moons which are called Phobos and Demos.

Jupiter is a huge ball of gas with a tiny dense core at the heart of it. The gas on the outer planets is mainly liquid hydrogen and helium with some methane and ethane. Uranus and Neptune may not have a core and it is possible that they are entirely composed of dust, swirling rocks and gas. (Odd to think that Neptune doesn't really exist and that Uranus is just a load of hot air!) Saturn, Uranus and Neptune all have ring systems and a number of Moons and smaller satellites orbiting them. Uranus goes about things in a very eccentric manner because it spins in the opposite direction to all the other planets and its poles are on the east and west rather than north and south. Uranus alternates between presenting its poles and its equator to the Sun so that each has a summer of forty-two years, followed by a forty-two-year winter.

Pluto has a very elongated orbit, part of which is inside the orbit of Neptune. It is too small to have any atmosphere, although frozen methane has been discovered on its surface. Pluto has one very large Moon called Charon which is about one third its size. Pluto and Charon could almost be called a binary planet system because one swings around the other, although Charon, being smaller, does more of the swinging than Pluto. The asteroid belt lies between Mars and Jupiter and is held in place by the gravity of the Sun on one side and of Jupiter on the other.

The Moon

The Moon's mean distance from the Earth, surface to surface, is 376,284 kilometres, or about a quarter of a million miles. It takes 27.32 days for the Moon to travel round the Earth and also 27.32 days for it to rotate on its axis, therefore it always has the same face pointing towards the Earth. Its diameter is 3475.6km and its temperature varies between plus 101 degrees and minus 153 degrees Celsius. The interior of the Moon is still hot enough to be made of molten rock and there are about 3,000 moonquakes per year. The surface of the Moon is fatter on the side which faces the Earth; it is also warmer on the Earth side. The Moon and the Earth were both formed when the Solar system came into being. The Moon became attracted to the Earth's gravitational field and formed a double or binary planet system. The Moon is about a quarter the size of the Earth and its surface area is about the size of Asia. Nevertheless its mountains reach 8,000 metres which is higher than any on earth. There is no atmosphere on the Moon.

Before the invention of modern telescope technology, only the Sun, Moon, Mercury, Venus, Mars, Jupiter and Saturn were known. Uranus was discovered by William Herschel in 1781, Neptune by John Adams and Urbain LeVerrier in 1846 and Pluto by Percival Lowell in 1930.

CHAPTER 3
Planetary Terminology

There are a number of planetary features on each individual chart which need to be taken into consideration in addition to their sign and house positions.

Personal, Transpersonal And Impersonal Planets

The personal planets are the Sun, Moon, Mercury, Venus and Mars. These are concerned with the personality and behaviour of the subject. The transpersonal planets are Jupiter and Saturn. These show how the subject copes with the opposing forces of expansion and limitation but they are slightly more concerned with external influences than personal behaviour. The outer planets of Uranus, Neptune and Pluto are the impersonal ones. These planets move so slowly that they have a group, or even a generational influence rather than a strictly personal one. For example, everybody who was born between June 1956 and August 1962 would have had Uranus in Leo, and would therefore all experience the energy of Uranus in much the same generational manner. (The connection between Leo and traditional fatherhood and the unruly nature of Uranus could count for the so-called 'generation gap' which was felt by people who were born during that time.) However, even these planets are never totally impersonal because everything in a birthchart makes itself felt. If a subject has a particularly difficult aspect to an impersonal natal planet, he would be aware of its effects, even if he knew nothing about astrology.

—————————**Retrograde Planets**—————————

A planet is said to be in retrograde motion when it appears to be travelling *backwards* along the ecliptic. It is not hard to become familiar with the position of planets in the sky overhead, because they tend to show themselves very clearly just before sunrise or after sunset. When you get used to their position, you will notice that they move a little from day to day, week to week or month to month. You will soon see that there are times when these planets go on a circular journey in the sky, moving backwards for a while before resuming their usual forward motion. This apparent backward motion is caused by the fact that the Earth is also travelling around the Sun and that all the planets are going at different speeds. It is a bit like travelling in a train and passing another which is moving in the same direction but more slowly. The slower train *appears* to be moving backwards.

Retrograde motion

From an astrologer's point of view, all the planets of the Solar system 'go retrograde' from time to time with the exception of the Sun and the Moon which are always in forward motion, and the nodes of the Moon which are always retrograde.

In a natal chart, if Mercury, Venus or Mars are retrograde, this will cause fairly obvious problems for the subject. Retrograde Jupiter and Saturn can also be difficult but the outer planets are not such a problem. When personal planets that are retrograde at birth move forward by progression, the problems which they cause in the natal chart can be seen to ease. When these planets are direct in the natal chart but turn retrograde by progression, the healthy state of the natal planet seems to offer protection.

Some people actually manage to work *with* their retrograde planets, whether these be retrograde natally or by progression, in order to take advantage of the windows of opportunity which are offered when these planets turn retrograde by *transit*. I know one person who has a natally retrograde Mercury and another who has had one for many years by progression and, untypically, both seem to find themselves buying large articles, particularly communications equipment and vehicles, when transitting Mercury is retrograde. They also make important commitments and sign contracts on a retrograde Mercury. These two ladies assure me that this is not a deliberate choice on their part, it just seems to work out that way for them.

———Exaltation, Detriment And Fall———

Planets are said to be comfortable when they are placed in their own sign; for example, Venus in Libra or the Sun in Leo. They are also comfortable when situated in their own houses, such as Mercury in the third or Jupiter in the ninth. However, there is also a series of really ancient placings which confer positive or negative vibes. The ancient list below covers only those planets which were known before the advent of modern astronomy.

Planet	*Exaltation*	*Fall*	*Detriment*
Sun	Aries	Libra	Aquarius
Moon	Taurus	Scorpio	Capricorn
Mercury	Virgo	Pisces	Sagittarius or Pisces
Venus	Pisces	Virgo	Scorpio or Aries
Mars	Capricorn	Cancer	Libra or Taurus
Jupiter	Cancer	Capricorn	Gemini or Virgo
Saturn	Libra	Aries	Cancer or Leo

While searching for further information on the exaltations, etc., I came across a small book written by Edwin Raphael in 1905 (published by Foulsham & Co Ltd). The following information is a modernised version of Mr Raphael's section on planetary attachments.

The most powerful attachment that the planets can have is to the signs and the houses that they rule. (There is more about this in the chapter which deals with the houses in detail.) They are influenced to a lesser extent by exaltation, detriment and fall. However, a planet which is exalted by the sign it occupies suggests that the subject could expect to rise 'far above his position at birth', presumably by using the particular energies of the planet, sign and house which are involved. Raphael goes even further to suggest *actual degrees* which are especially beneficial rather than the signs as a whole!

The Sun	19° Aries
The Moon	3° Taurus
Mercury	15° Virgo
Venus	27° Pisces
Mars	28° Capricorn
Jupiter	15° Cancer
Saturn	21° Libra

If a planet is opposite its sign of exaltation, it is in its fall and, therefore, somewhat unfortunate or unlucky in its effect. Planets which are opposite the signs they rule are in detriment, and these are supposed to be even more unfortunate in their effects. A typical situation would be Mars in Libra (Mars rules Aries which is opposite Libra).

This may seem to be an old-fashioned theory but if you have time to try it out on a few charts you will find that it works, especially when planets are within a degree or two of the points of exaltation. You will find a table at the back of this book which shows all the planetary attachments and influences in one place.

The Ruling Planet

The ruling planet is the one which is connected to the sign on the ascendant. For example, on a chart with Cancer rising, the ruling planet is the Moon, while on a chart with Scorpio rising, this would be Pluto, although Mars would need to be taken into consideration as well because it was the ruler of Scorpio before Pluto was discovered. The sign and house that the ruling planet occupies is important both natally and when it is affected by progressions and transits. Thus, if a subject with Libra rising experiences a transit of Uranus to his natal Venus, his life could be expected to change in a particularly dramatic manner. In addition to this, a birthchart with Libra or Taurus rising would have a strongly Venusian feel to it and the subject would have a Venusian approach to life. (For more information on everything to do with the ascendant, see my book *Rising Signs*.)

The Rising Planet

Some astrologers consider the rising planet to be the first one which appears after the ascendant. An obvious rising planet would be one which appeared in the first house. If there are no planets in the first house then the first planet to appear in the second or third house would be the rising planet. Other astrologers consider the rising planet to be the first one appearing *above the eastern horizon*. If you bear in mind that the upper half of the birthchart, that is, the half which is comprised of the seventh, eighth, ninth, tenth, eleventh and twelfth houses, represents daylight and the lower half night, then the first planet above the eastern horizon is in *the twelfth house*.

Most astrologers would be happy to call any planet which is close to the ascendant a rising planet. The rising planet will have a bearing on the subject's early life and will tend to be a strong influence throughout his life. For example, Saturn rising will encourage the subject to think things out for himself and to choose a profession or a lifestyle where self-discipline, a thorough knowledge of his subject and the ability to concentrate on details and to work alone come in handy. According to the French statistician, Michel Gauquelin, surgeons tend to have this placement, while I have discovered that many writers also have Saturn close to the ascendant.

There are cases where there is no rising planet because all the planets are grouped together well away from the ascendant.

——————Mutual Reception——————

Two planets are in mutual reception when they are in each other's signs; for example, the Moon in Taurus and Venus in Cancer, or the Sun in Sagittarius and Jupiter in Leo. There is always a strong connection between these planets and they can express two sides of a personality which are linked. The Sagittarius/Leo combination indicates royalty which suggests that the subject may indeed have royal blood or he may just act as though he does! There may be a particular attitude which is expressed through this mutual reception. For example, a man with the Moon in Scorpio and Mars in Cancer may see every woman as a combination of a saint and a whore.

——————Unaspected Planets——————

In theory, these planets should 'disappear' from a birthchart and have a very weak impact in the subject's life. In fact, the subject may strive to develop the very area which is apparently missing. My astrologer friend, Maggie Hyde, has an unaspected Mercury in Pisces yet she writes for magazines, has recently had her first book published and runs a school of astrology. I have an unaspected Neptune, yet I have worked in every kind of Neptunian field, including a prison and a mental hospital, and am very interested in anything of an artistic or psychic nature.

——————The Leading Planet——————

Some birthcharts have a clutch of planets in one area. The first of this group of planets is said to be the leading planet. I don't consider this to have any special importance on the chart except perhaps when a planet crosses it by transit, because the transit will touch off a train of events which will be played out as each planet in turn is crossed by the transitting one.

————————Midpoints————————

Midpoints are the halfway point between two planets or between a planet and the ascendant, the midheaven or any other sensitive point on a birthchart. Midpoints are not difficult to calculate but doing so is a time-consuming job; however, a computer does the job in no time.

There are so many midpoints that it would be impossible to interpret them all. The best approach is to get your computer to sort out the midpoints by *sign* and then print them out. Then you should look down the list for a sign which has a large number of midpoints in it, and then look at the effects of transits to these areas over a period of time. Recently, a client of mine seemed to be responding strongly to the conjunction of Uranus and Neptune in Capricorn yet she had no planets in either Cancer or Capricorn (or for that matter in Aries or Libra either). However, her midpoint chart showed plenty going on in Cancer, hence her response to the activity going on in the opposite sign of Capricorn. Another client has important midpoints at three degrees of two different signs and she reacts whenever any transitting planet reaches three degrees of any sign.

————————What Goes Round Which?————————

The first thing any of us learns about astrology is our Sun sign. This simply refers to the sign the Sun appeared to be passing through at the time of our birth. In fact, we know that it is the Earth which moves around the Sun against the backdrop of the stars which appear to pass along the ecliptic but, because astrologers still tend to look at the sky as the ancients did, our charts assume that it is the Sun which is doing the travelling.

────Heliocentric charts────

It is possible to work out horoscopes as though we were standing on the surface of the Sun instead of the Earth. This kind of astrology is called heliocentric astrology whilst normal astrology is geocentric. ('Helios' is Greek for the Sun, while 'geo' is Greek for anything which refers to the Earth. Geocentric, therefore, means centred on the Earth.)

If you have access to a computer program which produces a heliocentric chart, take a look at it because it is very interesting. There is a great deal missing from these charts which makes what is left especially powerful. For example, there are no astrological houses. Every chart is 'natural', which means that it has zero degrees of Aries where the ascendant would normally be. The Sun is replaced by the Earth but this is placed exactly opposite to where the Sun would be on a geocentric chart. There is no Moon, no node and no part of fortune.

Looking at the signs as if they were houses on a heliocentric chart can provide interesting interpretations. Check out planets in Libra or Scorpio for relationships, Cancer and Capricorn for parents, Leo for children, Taurus for possessions and personal values and so on. Does your Earth sign represent a past life or the next life or, maybe, the life you would like to have? The Earth sign may represent the Sun sign you would like to have been born with. Do the planets represent people in your life, or just the way you are? Do some research on this for yourself, you may come up with some good ideas. Having tried out this method on a number of charts, I am convinced that Mars denotes the querent's father, and Mercury, the mother. I tried out a number of people who all considered that they had had diabolical childhoods with really dreadful mothers and in every case, Mercury turned up in Scorpio! Incidentally, all of these subjects had very enquiring minds and were hard to influence.

CHAPTER 4

An Introduction to the Planets

This chapter includes a synopsis of each planet's meaning which should provide a *handle*; that is, something to grasp when looking at a chart. The next chapter deals with the planets in depth but this chapter provides an introductory digest which will help the beginner to get started. Each synopsis is followed by a list which includes all the ideas commonly associated with each planet and also the less well-known ones. This can be used both by beginners and experienced astrologers alike as a quick and easy reference.

The Sun

The sign the Sun occupies is vitally important. The Sun represents all that we *create* and *project*, whether this be our own nature, the creation of a child or any kind of enterprise or lifestyle. The desire to create a happy home is a Sun matter. A decision to *do* anything, or to take an active part in anything is a Sun sign matter. The Sun is associated with success and achievement, the fun side of life and all that makes life worth living.

The following items are all associated with the Sun

1 The personality and general outlook on life
2 Winning, succeeding, achieving
3 Creativity in all senses of the word
4 Children

5 Fathers or father figures
6 Business, especially if it is successful or glamorous
7 Show business, glamorous professions and lifestyles
8 Entertainments, holidays, amusements, games and, to some extent, gambling and games of chance
9 Music
10 Love affairs. These can be amusing diversions or deeply felt affections but they are supposed to be fun, even if they don't always feel like it at the time.

The Moon

The Moon symbolises the way we *feel*, and this encompasses far more than our emotional life or our personal relationships. For instance, a subject may have a wonderful job but he may *feel* unhappy about it. The Sun *acts* but the Moon *reacts* and this intuitive, reactive response is often the right one. The Moon rules our habits and our behaviour when ill, drunk or otherwise uninhibited. It represents our experience of being nurtured and our capacity to nurture others and it is associated with the home and any property or premises which we utilise.

The following items are all associated with the Moon

1 Inner feelings, emotions and emotional reactions, habitual behaviour and the way we are when ill, drunk or otherwise being our real selves
2 Real inner needs such as ambition, love, revenge or any other personal motivation and driving force — however well disguised
3 Mothers or mother figures, the experience of being nurtured
4 The home. Premises or property. The domestic scene. Also small shops or businesses that are run on a personal basis and are the subject's own territory.

 5 Women, female matters
 6 The public
 7 Some health matters, especially chronic ones and those
   brought on by unhappiness
 8 Travel and restlessness
 9 Moods and changeability
10 Sailors and sewing (sailors were skilled at sewing sails,
   nets, sacks, clothing and so on)
11 Dairymaids, cows
12 The cooking and storage of food, thus the larder, fridge,
   cooker, implements and, of course, the cook
13 Attachment to the past, patriotism, interest in history and
   collecting things which have a history to them, such as
   antiques

————————————Mercury————————————

Mercury rules thought, words, communications and knowledge.
It is associated with local matters, travel and transport and
movement of goods and ideas. Negotiations, paperwork and
education are ruled by Mercury. Mercury also denotes brothers
and sisters and neighbours. A fair amount of the kind of things
we all have to do as part of normal daily life are associated with
Mercury.

The following items are all associated with Mercury

1 Communications
2 Travel and transport
3 Local matters, the neighbourhood
4 Knowledge. Primary and secondary education
5 The mind, the mental processes, the way one thinks
6 Brothers and sisters, cousins and similar relationships
7 Youthfulness
8 Health and healing
9 Magic

10 Sales and marketing
11 Thieves and theft
12 Rail and bus termini. Boundary markers (Latin = *hermi* probably from the Greek name of Hermes for the Roman god, Mercury)

Venus

Venus is associated with the things we hold dear to us. This includes material possessions, land and also concepts such as our values and priorities. Venus is very much associated with sensuality, in short, anything which appeals to the senses. This includes music and art, dancing, food, sex, fresh air and anything else which *feels* good and does us good. We can be very attached to the things which we own or enjoy and therefore, Venus shows what we will fight to keep. This planet is also associated with relationships which are open to scrutiny. This could mean a husband or a close associate but it can just as easily concern an open and acknowledged enemy. Mars may represent the way we go to war but Venus could represent the person we fight and the reasons for the battle.

The following items are all associated with Venus

1 Values and priorities
2 Valuable goods and personal possessions. Personal finances
3 Love, romance and sexuality
4 Leisure and pleasure
5 Music and art
6 Ostentation and luxury
7 Females
8 Emotions connected to love and possessions
9 Open friendships and relationships such as marriage
10 Open enemies. The reason for fighting
11 Mirrors, decorative glass, venetian blinds. (Venice is the city of Venus and, presumably the home of venetian

blinds. The Venetians still make wonderful glass ornaments today.)

12 Cosmetics, powder compacts (with and without mirrors)
13 Sea shells, flowers, oysters
14 Aphrodisiacs and venereal diseases (although AIDS comes under the rulership of Pluto)
15 Copper, malachite (which is copper ore), emeralds
16 Justice and fair play. Legal arguments
17 Balance, harmony

———————————Mars———————————

Mars denotes energy and drive which can be used positively or negatively. On one hand, Mars adds assertiveness, courage and sexuality to a personality but it can add aggression, violence and danger. Too much Mars is much like too much adrenalin or too much testosterone! Just the right amount gives a subject the heart to fight when the time is right. This planet is not concerned with actual possessions and material objects in the way that Venus is but it may be used to get them.

The following items are all associated with Mars

1 Energy, assertiveness, forcefulness, initiative, etc.
2 Passion, the desire for something
3 The drive to obtain the person or the object of one's desire
4 Decision-making and decisive action
5 Arguments and violence
6 Masculine occupations such as engineering, steel making and (with Pluto) coal mining
7 Competitive activities, especially sports
8 Iron and steel, surgical instruments. Tools, especially knives, blades
9 Warfare, weapons, the tools of destruction
10 Blood

—Jupiter—

Jupiter signifies expansion and exploration. Anything which pushes back boundaries, surmounts barriers and creates opportunities is ruled by Jupiter. There are some specific areas which are outlined in the list below but the general idea is to take a concept, a desire or an opportunity and run with it as far as one can go. Jupiter can destroy in order that something better is built after the destruction.

The following items are all associated with Jupiter

1 Foreign travel or exploration of new places
2 The law and the legal system
3 Belief, religion and philosophy
4 What a subject believes in and feels strongly about
5 Education, especially higher education
6 Money, business and success in these fields
7 Opportunities. Meeting new and influential people
8 Publishing and broadcasting
9 Large animals. Outdoor life and sporting activities
10 Gambling and winning. (Traditionally, horse racing)

—Saturn—

Saturn is blamed for all our ills but this is unfair. Saturn may be a task-master but he helps us to reach our goals and to pick up the rewards of our efforts. Saturn does rule difficult circumstances and times of restriction or limitation but these help to build character and strength of personality. This planet presides over craftsmanship and attention to detail, and ultimate success through hard work and persistence.

The following items are all associated with Saturn

1 Endurance, persistence, restraint, caution
2 Self-discipline, organisation, time sense

3 Ambition, success which is well deserved
4 Maturity, senior citizenship, old age
5 Some aspects of pain and suffering, especially if the situation is lasting or chronic
6 Banking, big business, large organisations
7 Structure and a firm foundation
8 Authority and status
9 Lead, pipes — especially household plumbing. Plumbers
10 Clocks, watches and time pieces of all kinds
11 Measuring instruments of all kinds, e.g. clocks, rulers, weights, slide rules, computers used for mathematical purposes. Calculations and, in ancient times, astrology!
12 Coffin makers
13 Masonry, building materials, the building trade
14 Taboos

Uranus

Uranus is more concerned with ideas than feelings, it is associated with group and political activities. However, Uranian people are hard to categorise and don't conform to any type of group or section of society. This is the planet of change, of revolution and of modern inventions and ideas of all kinds. Uranus rules friendship and other detached relationships.

The following items are all associated with Uranus

1 Groups and political activities, especially green or humanitarian ones
2 Idealism, humanitarianism, any other 'ism' which benefits the group rather than the individual
3 Individualism, independence, self-motivation
4 Ideas, concepts
5 Technical innovation and inventions which may or may not change the world
6 Shocks and surprises — some nice, some nasty, but all enlightening
7 Obstinacy and eccentricity

—————————————**Neptune**—————————————

Neptune rules the greatest that we can aspire to and the lowest levels of degradation. It brings confusion and loss but also love of the purest and most romantic kind. This planet presides over the creation of illusion for entertainment such as in films and music and also illusions brought on by strange moods, alcohol and drugs.

The following items are all associated with Neptune

1 Illusion of both the good and bad kinds
2 Appreciation of things other than the basic needs of food, clothing and shelter
3 Love of God and religious or mystical revelations
4 Romantic love, especially when one endows the lover with more character and attributes than he actually has
5 Creativity, especially if the creation depends upon illusion, as in film
6 Shifting sands, nothing being what it seems, lies, deception and self-deception
7 The sea and fishing
8 Travel to or over water. Holidays on or by water (or snow)
9 Gas, smells, perfume, anaesthetics
10 Alcohol and drugs
11 Glass, especially when used in a functional rather than in a decorative manner. For example, in spectacles, microscopes, telescopes, and so on
12 Photography and film
13 Self-sacrifice, social work, doing things for others
14 Places of seclusion such as hospitals, prisons and mental institutions. Also the workers and the work that is associated with these places. Also voluntary workers

─────────────────────Pluto─────────────────────

Pluto rules the birth, death or transformation of anything. Also, committed sexual partnerships and joint financial arrangements. It denotes important financial matters, particularly where other people are involved. It presides over things which are hidden from the eye and the means of uncovering or extracting these. Most of all it symbolises transformation and the collective unconscious.

The following items are all associated with Pluto

1 Birth and death, especially death. The passage to the 'other side'
2 Transformation, recycling, changing from one state to another
3 Sex, procreation and committed relationships
4 Wills, legacies, taxes, accountancy on behalf of others
5 Business matters related to money, stocks and shares, insurance. Business commitments
6 Mining, excavation, archaeology
7 Butchery, surgery, cutting with knives
8 Psychiatry, unlocking the unconscious
9 Investigation, espionage, counter espionage
10 Engineering, military matters, macho images
11 Power broking, power behind the scenes, manipulation

─────────────The nodes of the Moon─────────────

The following items are all associated with the nodes of the Moon*

1 North node: Where we are going, karmically
    South node: Where we have come from, karmically
2 North node: How we fit into current social and political thinking
    South node: How our desires differ from 'political correctness' or from the society that we live in

* You will find a full explanation of the nodes in Chapter 5.

3 North node: Something beneficial to do with property
  South node: Same as north node but this may relate to
  the past in some way
4 North node: Future
  South node: Past

CHAPTER 5
The Planets in Detail

Each planet has a personality of its own which is expressed in different ways according to the sign and house it occupies. It is also influenced by the aspects which are made to it by other planets. Any of the factors outlined in chapter 4 will have some kind of impact on the way each planet expresses itself.

I have broken down the analysis of each planet into sections showing the most popular and widely understood interpretations, followed by the other, less well-known, subsidiary meanings.

THE SUN

The sun whose rays are all ablaze
With ever living glory,
Does not deny his majesty
He scorns to tell a story,
He don't exclaim
'I blush for shame
So kindly be indulgent',
But fierce and bold
In fiery gold, he glories all effulgent.

I mean to rule the earth as he the sky,
We really know our worth, the sun and I.
From *The Mikado* by Gilbert and Sullivan

The Sun rules the sign of Leo and the fifth house of the zodiac. In Roman mythology, it is associated with the god, Apollo.

When trying to explain the active nature of the Sun, and the reactive nature of the Moon to students, I usually give this little example. A person makes a decision to go and buy something new and interesting, but when he gets to the shop there is a queue. While waiting in the queue, someone pushes in front of him. The decision to go shopping is an active one which belongs to the Sun while his reaction to finding a queue and deciding to wait in line is a Lunar one. He may react to the queue-jumper by sighing gently and making room for him, or he may become aggressive. Either reaction would depend upon the state of the person's Moon both natally and by progression and transit at the time of the event.

First Principles

The Sun is the largest and most obvious object in the sky so it is no surprise that it exerts a very strong influence on our birthcharts. This is fortunate for those of us who write Sun sign features in papers and magazines because the strength of this 'planet' and the heavy emphasis on the sign it occupies makes our job just about viable. However, there are plenty of people who say that they are nothing like their Sun sign, due to strongly modifying factors on their charts. Traditional teaching, however, says that the Sun signifies the self and that it has a strong influence on a subject's character and behaviour. To some extent this is true even for those who aren't typical of their sign; the story below illustrates this point.

Some years ago my husband had a friend with a timid, pale and silent wife called Pauline. Unbelievably, Pauline was a Leo. Whenever we went out with this couple my heart sank because I knew I would be expected to entertain Pauline, and I found her almost impossible to talk to. Her life was very humdrum, she had nothing to say and there was virtually no common ground between us. One day we went to their house for dinner and out of desperation I asked her about her four children, all of whom were in some form of higher education. She took me to an amazing room at the back of the small house. This room contained just about every educational toy, game or book imaginable. Shelves were stacked to overflowing with boxed sets of things which had been bought over a period of many years. This Leo lady then began to talk about her children's education and development in a most animated manner. She had obviously directed every ounce of her considerable Leonine pride and psychic energy into these children. All her boring pointless 'little' jobs were designed for one purpose only, to provide the wherewithal for these children to *win*, *win win*. I have lost touch with Pauline now but I expect one day to come across her children in Parliament, making a fortune on the stock exchange or officiating as high court judges.

The moral of this story is that even the most atypical person has a core of their Sun sign personality hidden away somewhere. It is also interesting that the second main significance of the Sun in a chart is *creativity*. Creativity takes many forms apart from the obvious one of making things with one's hands. One can create a business, a beautiful home or, of course, a family, so the fact that Pauline chose her children as the vehicle for her Leonine pride and creativity was not, after all, so surprising.

————————Subsidiary Definitions————————

The Sun can throw some light on the relationship between fathers and children and vice versa. Some astrologers actually see the Sun as the father in the chart while others, through the Sun's rulership of the fifth house and the sign of Leo, see it as being associated with children. It may be that the Sun works in either direction, showing the relationship to the father at some times in life and to the children at others.

Although not specifically associated with health, the condition of the Sun in a birthchart can show whether a subject is likely to be healthy or ailing. A badly-aspected natal Sun could indicate poor health. It could also indicate repression by others, particularly during childhood and especially by a father or father figure. A sad and repressed person is likely to suffer from ill-health, so the two ideas are linked.

The Sun sign determines the strength of a subject's personality and how he chooses to live his life, his leadership qualities — or lack of them — and his ability to exert power and authority. It can be connected with business matters or wheeling and dealing of various kinds. For example, a person with a well-aspected Sun in Aries near the mid-heaven would make a successful politician.

Through the association with Leo, the Sun is supposed to denote how we spend our leisure time, showing the kind of holidays we take and the things which give us pleasure. Love affairs, sporting activities, gambling, games of chance and amusements of all kinds are attributed to the Sun. This can be a bit confusing because the planet, Venus, is also associated with leisure and pleasure. Perhaps both apply, with some things pleasing the more masculine Sun aspect of our personalities and others appealing to the feminine Venusian aspect.

Another interest which is both Solar and Venusian is music. The Sun god in Roman mythology was Apollo and he, of course, was the god of music. The difference between the two planets is that, while Venus is in it for pleasure alone, the Sun wants to shine. Strong Sun subjects are competitive and want to look good, to be successful and to stand out in a crowd. However, playfulness, childlike behaviour and the pursuit of fun and amusement for its own sake are also Solar interests.

Something which is often forgotten is that the Sun can be associated with successful business ventures. Once again, it is the creative side of such enterprises which comes under the province of the Sun. A business, especially a small one, is a very creative enterprise, often the manifestation of somebody's personal vision. If the Sun shines on a business venture, it is sure to be a success. I have already mentioned that Apollo was the god of music, so the Sun presides over all forms of music, entertainment and show business. Even the showbiz side of sports would come under this category.

The Sun rules anything which glistens, therefore jewellery, especially that made from gold, is a Sun related matter. Into this category come glamorous clothes, glamorous people and fascinating, star-studded events. The entertainment business is associated with a number of planets such as Neptune for films, Venus for singing and Jupiter for comedy, but the industry in general, with its creativity and the fun and pleasure, lives under the rule of the Sun.

THE MOON

Observe night's flame, that placid dame,
The moon's celestial highness,
There's not a trace upon her face
Of diffidence or shyness,
She borrows light that through the night,
Mankind may all acclaim her,
And truth to tell she lights up well,
So I for one don't blame her.

I pray make no mistake, we are not shy,
We're very wide awake, the moon and I.

From *The Mikado* by Gilbert and Sullivan

The Moon rules the sign of Cancer and the fourth house. It has many mythological connections, my favourite being that of Persephone, the daughter of Demeter who was the goddess of agriculture. I'm sure you remember the story of Demeter and Persephone, but I'll remind you anyway. Pluto, the god of the underworld, took a strong fancy to Persephone and commanded her to come and live with him under the ground for a while. Not only had Persephone to go and stay with Pluto but she had to go without food or drink while she was there — otherwise she would be trapped there forever. Persephone tried dieting for a few days and then, like all dieters, hunger got the better of her. She ate six pomegranate seeds and Pluto insisted that she could not leave. Her mother, Demeter, was so upset that she went on strike until he returned her daughter. The upshot was that Demeter and Pluto reached a compromise, so that the Earth would not die. Persephone was punished with a six-month sentence during which time she had to stay with him in Hades. Not only that, but the sentence was repeated each year. Demeter responded by going into mourning for each of the six-month periods. And that, according to mythology, is why we have six months of growth and six months of decline in agriculture each year!

————————First Principles————————

The Moon is traditionally associated with the emotions, inner feelings and underlying urges. Ancient astrologers considered the Moon to be restless because of her rapid movement through the sky and therefore attributed her to changeability, emotional feelings and moods. The Moon shows how a subject reacts to situations and how he behaves when his passions are aroused. Some of this instinctive behaviour refers back to childhood and it may also have some karmic significance. The underlying Lunar personality will reveal itself when the subject is tired, ill or overwrought. It shows the subject's ability to adapt to a situation and also his obsessions and deepest needs. For example, a woman with the Moon in Aries would find it hard to fit into a 'me Tarzan, you Jane' type of marriage. A person with the Moon in Sagittarius might tackle a difficult situation by escaping. A Moon-Sagittarius friend of mine got out of a really awful marriage by behaving pleasantly to her husband until she was good and ready to leave and then hiring a moving van and doing a 'flit'.

Traditional astrology associates the Moon with mother figures and one's first experience of being nurtured, whether by one's own mother or by someone else. Some more contemporary astrologers consider the Moon to be the child within the subject. I see no problem with any of this because astrological symbols can be read on a variety of different levels. (Remember the powerful mother/ daughter connection in the Demeter/Persephone legend.) One could take the simplistic view of looking at the Moon as the mother on the chart and then go over it again looking for the 'Jungian' child within. If, for instance, a subject's Moon was in Libra in the fourth house, he would probably have a peaceful relationship with a mother who is nice-looking, pleasant and home-loving. However, the cardinality of Libra and the angularity of the fourth house would mean that she was no pushover and that she liked being in charge of her home and her children. If we now look at the Moon as the child within the subject, he would want a peaceful, good and secure home life where he could both be looked after and, at the same time, be in charge of the situation. He might run his business or his office as if it were a family, enjoying that family feeling of looking after the employees. He might even be a union leader. The scenarios here are pure invention but they show how this idea of mother/child and the child within us works. Many astrologers feel that most of us are more like our Moon sign when young and that we only become like our Sun sign after the Saturn return at the age of twenty-nine.

The Moon is associated with the home both in the sense of domestic harmony and also more practical matters, such as buying, leasing or renting property or premises. These premises may not, strictly speaking, be for living in but rather for work, renting out or keeping as a holiday home. The property aspect of the Moon is probably more important when looking at progressions and transits than in a natal chart where the feelings associated with *home life* are more important.

A well-placed Moon should assure a secure and happy childhood but the rest of the chart would have to confirm this. Even if the rest of the chart shows areas of difficulty, a comfortable Moon will be a great help to the subject.

————Subsidiary Definitions————

The Moon's position and condition can define a subject's attitude to the feminine. It also denotes whether or not women's issues are an important factor in a subject's life. If you are looking at any of this on a chart, you should look at Venus as well as the Moon.

I find it hard to reconcile the Moon's association with the public because it seems to be so firmly tied to the private aspect of life. However, the north node of the Moon can show where and how a person fits in with the public mood, and a strong tenth or eleventh house Moon would be ideal for someone who wants to do something for the public good.

The Moon is not specifically associated with health but it can show up a weak area in a subject's body. One's state of mind, one's emotional state and one's health are so often linked that this is not really surprising. Chronic ailments such as rheumatism, migraine and bronchitis are typical of the kind of ailments which are exacerbated by Lunar unhappiness.

Earlier astrology books link the Moon with the sea and with travel. This seems to work very well because people who have the Moon in signs or houses which are associated with travel do move around quite a lot. Early astrology books also suggested that someone with the Moon in the ninth house could marry a foreigner. My friend, Nina, has the Moon in the ninth house in Pisces. Nina is a native New Yorker who visited London for a holiday, met the man who was to become her husband, and has subsequently made her home here. Many people with the Moon in the ninth house are drawn to astrology and the esoteric, and Nina is an aromatherapist, clairvoyant, astrologer, palmist and aura reader.

Incidentally, I have noticed that people who have the Moon in air signs or houses are particularly restless, spending their lives travelling, often in connection with work.

────────── The Moon's Nodes ──────────

The nodes of the Moon are the points at which the Moon crosses the ecliptic each month. To demystify this statement, the ecliptic is the path that the Sun and the planets appear to follow around the Earth. We all know how the Solar system works, but from our viewing point on Earth, the Sun and the visible planets *appear* to be travelling around us. The only thing which actually *does* travel around the Earth is the Moon, and this takes a steeper (more up and down) path than the ecliptic. This means that the Moon crosses the ecliptic in an upwards direction once a month and then back across it in a downwards direction just under two weeks later.

The point where the Moon crosses the ecliptic on the upwards journey is called the north node while the point where it crosses on its downwards journey is called the south node. The position of the two nodes each month moves slightly backwards along the ecliptic so, from the point of view of astrologers, they are always in retrograde motion. This never alters, although the movement against the ecliptic can vary a little over a period of time. The position of the north node is given in every ephemeris, whether this be the large kind which covers a century, or the annual kind, such as, *Raphael's Ephemeris*. The south node is always directly opposite the north node, thus a north node at 14 degrees of Libra means that the south node must be at 14 degrees of Aries.

Three ways of looking at the nodes

From an astrologer's point of view, the nodes are both interesting and important. There seem to be three ways of looking at them. First and foremost, many astrologers consider that they have some relationship with the pattern of karma and reincarnation. Indian astrologers refer to the north node as the dragon's head (Rahu) and the south node as the dragon's tail (Kethu). Their idea is that the south node represents our previous lives and all that we have learned so far. We are supposed to find the area of life which the south node occupies easy to deal with, while we struggle to come to terms with *this* life's lessons, which are represented by the north node. Flipping casually through my file of famous people's charts, I have picked the following at random:

1 The Duchess of York: South node in Aries, north node in Libra. Lessons about relationships, perhaps?
2 Prince Charles: South node in Scorpio, north node in Taurus. He is at home with the deeper aspects of life and is, of course a Sun in Scorpio subject. He must learn to be more practical, to cope with financial matters and to work out what is valuable to him and to others. He may need to learn how to relate on a personal level too.
3 Margaret Thatcher: South node in Aquarius, north node in Leo. She is at ease when dealing with groups, working in the political field and changing the world but she needs to learn creativity and development of the self. This is a very idealistic placement.

A second and very interesting interpretation of the nodes is that the north node is attuned to the general atmosphere which is currently prevailing in society. To clarify this statement; when a planet transits the north node, we seem to do things which fit in with the general outlook of people around us; we are *politically correct* and are respected by the world for the rightness of our behaviour. An important transit to the south node might put us against the general trend and make us appear rebellious and out of tune with the views of others. An example of this might be of two women who have both decided to start new businesses. One chooses to open a health food shop with a healing centre attached while the other opens a furriers. Which business was 'politically correct' in the socio-economic climate of the mid-1990s? What are the chances of financial success in each case?

If you look at the transits of the nodes in the ephemeris, in addition to looking at progressions and transits of other planets to your own nodes, you will be surprised at how important they are. The best transit is a trine or sextile to the north node because this inevitably brings a sextile or trine to the south node at the same time. A conjunction to one node inevitably brings an opposition to the other one. The worst scenario is a square because both nodes become involved in a 'T square'. Another difficult one is a semi-sextile to one node and an inconjunct to the other.

The Moon itself has some connection with the past, so previous experiences and past-life experiences do seem to have relevance when looking at the nodes. For example, there could be some change in connection with a subject's mother, home, emotional state, family or anything else which is represented by the Moon, particularly if this is linked with the past in some way. In my experience as an astrologer, the most frequent events of this kind seem to be connected to property and premises or family life, but some people begin important enterprises on significant node transits.

Minor transits to the nodes indicate trivial events such as going on holiday, having visitors or decorating and renovating the home. I recently renewed an acquaintance with some old friends and have since visited them on a regular basis. I noticed that a number of planets were aspecting my nodes when this happened. 'Should auld acquaintance be forgot' — look up your old nodes!

MERCURY

A wandering minstrel I,
A thing of shreds and patches,
Of ballads, songs and snatches
Of dreamy lullaby.
My catalogue is long
Through every passion ranging,
And to your humours changing
I tune my supple song.

From *The Mikado* by Gilbert and Sullivan

Mercury rules Gemini and Virgo, the third and sixth houses of the chart. The Roman god, Mercury, was the messenger of the gods and when required, he ran their dirty-tricks department. Mercury was also associated with medicine, magic and thieves!

————————**First Principles**————————

Mercury rules all forms of communication, therefore it is associated with speech, thought, writing and messages of all kinds, including those which travel through the body's nervous system. In modern life, Mercury is associated with telephones, faxes, computer modems and all forms of the communications media. Due to the concept of message-carrying, Mercury traditionally rules local travel and transport. However, the world is metaphorically so small nowadays, that local could actually mean to the other side of — and even far above — the Earth. Therefore, taxis, couriers and also world-wide postal, parcel services and messages passed on via satellites through the telephone and television systems would be ruled by Mercury.

By the beginning of this century, most countries had been explored to some extent but many people all over the world seldom left their own villages. Nowadays, ordinary citizens think nothing of travelling to the other side of the world in the space of a few hours, so one could put all normal forms of travel under the rule of Mercury. I suggest that you either use Mercury to indicate travel within one's own country and Jupiter for overseas travel, or, alternatively, that you assign all normal forms of travel and transport to Mercury and only use Jupiter for journeys of exploration. The choice is yours.

Anything which requires skill is typically Mercurial, therefore craftwork, light engineering, dressmaking and the use of office machinery all come into this category. Mercury signifies knowledge, teaching and learning. Traditional astrology suggests that Mercury rules primary, secondary and further education while Jupiter rules higher education. Language learning is particularly Mercurial, as is computer programming. You can include any means of passing on information such as overhead projectors, video tapes and good old-fashioned conversation in this category. Mercury rules the mind, the ability to think on one's feet and to cope with everyday life in a normal manner. A well-placed Mercury denotes the ability to learn and to communicate but, if it is badly-placed, there would be difficulties in this area. A friend of mine has come across a number of dyslexic people who all had retrograde Mercuries close to their ascendants. I once had a neighbour who was a teacher with a mentally-handicapped daughter whose birthday was 6th April 1966. During her teaching career, she found herself teaching a class of children, all of whom were born during 1965 and 1966. Three of these children had been born on the same day as her daughter and all three of them had learning difficulties. The children had Mercuries which were in exact conjunction with Saturn in Scorpio. In the case of my neighbour's daughter, this conjunction was in the twelfth house, close to her Scorpio ascendant.

Mercury, being the *local* planet, is associated with one's immediate neighbourhood and, therefore, rules anything to do with neighbours, local shops, schools and anything else that is nearby. This includes places that are habitually visited such as the area around a subject's place of work and anywhere else that he or she is closely involved with. A well-aspected Mercury would suggest living in an area of friendly neighbours, good local facilities and a happy environment, while a badly-aspected Mercury could bring the agony of living close to difficult neighbours or in an unpleasant neighbourhood. Mercury in the fourth house, Cancer or an earth sign could suggest working in or near home or staying in the same house or the same place of work for a long time.

Mercury is also associated with brothers, sisters and anyone else with whom a subject was brought up. Cousins or other relatives of one's own age would qualify, as would close relationships with colleagues, friends and associates, especially if they live nearby.

—————Subsidiary Definitions—————

Mercury is associated with young people and all the things they like to do. It is considered to be a fairly androgynous planet but I tend to think of it as young and male. Youthful interests such as sport, pop music, keeping up with the latest fashions and getting together for a gossip fit well here. Mercurial people tend to stay young at heart even when they get old. Mercury is also reputed to represent the 'Peter Pan' person who never really wants to grow up and who fears old age. Some astrologers make a real meal of this but I'm not so sure; most of the Mercurial people whom I have come across are young at heart but they also have a responsible attitude to life.

Mercury is very much associated with health and healing, especially when the hands are used to diagnose or to heal. The Roman god's symbol was the caduceus, or herald's wand, and this is still used as a healing symbol today, but the asteroid, Chiron, is also concerned with health and healing in astrology. Along with healing, Mercury is associated with magic and it is quite easy to see why. In the past, and even now in primitive cultures, magic rituals, shamanism and healing are closely linked. A spiritual healer must be able to open his chakras, tap into the energy of the universe and use his hands in order to work the magic of healing. Good doctors, dentists and therapists all have a kind of magic in their personalities which inspires trust and helps their patients to help themselves.

Mercury rules sales and marketing and many aspects of the day-to-day running of any business. This is great if everything is honest and above board, but remember that Mercury also rules trickery and sharp practice.

My astrologer friend, Jonathan Dee, reminded me that tradition places Mercury as the god of thieves and that this planet's position on a chart can show where a subject is likely to lose out through theft or trickery during his life. There is an element both of concealment and revelation about this strange planet which has to be experienced before it can be understood. Mercury was the god who guided the dead to the underworld and therefore he is the link between this world and the next. He seems to know more than he is prepared to reveal to us, at least until the right time, and therefore is both wiser and trickier than we realise. Mercury is adept at prevarication, half-truths and the kind of concealment situation where one knows for sure that something is going on, and where one cannot or should not talk about it! Professional astrological consultants usually take a leaf from Mercury's book and make value judgements about when to speak up and when to keep quiet during a reading because Mercury can be the god of when *not* to communicate!

VENUS

If you go in, you're sure to win
Yours will be the charming lady.
Be your law the ancient saw,
Faint heart never won fair lady.
While the sun shines make your hay
Where a will is, there's a way
Beard the lion in his lair,
None but the brave deserve the fair!
Nothing ventured nothing win,
Blood is thick but water's thin
In for a penny, in for a pound,
It's love that makes the world go round!

From *Iolanthe* by Gilbert and Sullivan

Venus rules Taurus and Libra, and the second and seventh houses. Venus was the Roman goddess of love and also of sexuality but seems to have lost some of her sexual connotations in modern astrology. Perhaps we will revive them here!

————————**First Principles**————————

Venus is associated with the things one values, especially material goods and personal finances. It used to be the fashion among spiritually-minded consultants to tell their clients to 'let go' of their nasty materialistic ways so that they could reach a 'higher level' of spirituality. I think there should be some balance between greed and need and I see nothing wrong in valuing what is possessed, whether it is a family heirloom which has been handed down or something for which one has worked hard. I also see nothing attractive about poverty! Venus's second house rulership states that the goods and finances in question belong to the subject *himself*, but the seventh house connection denotes that these could be used to attract a partner or to make a partner's life comfortable (or vice versa). The partner's wealth is *not* a Venusian matter; other people's money is ruled by Pluto and, possibly, also by Mars.

The 'value' aspects of Venus can include valuing time to oneself, or valuing such concepts as freedom or security. The things that one considers to be important are ruled by Venus as are one's self-esteem and self-value. If having one's windows cleaned, saving for a holiday or spending a day fixing the car are priorities, then these too are ruled by Venus.

Venus, of course, was the Roman goddess of love. We tend to see this nowadays as romantic love, the kind which makes one's head spin and one's heart ache, but in the old days, Venus was seen as a very sexual being and the temple maidens who were dedicated to her were very far from being 'Vestal Virgins'. Transits to Venus can produce a sudden rush of 'hearts and flowers' romance and/or a true passion of a very sexual nature. Venusian love puts the loved one on a pedestal but it can also signify greed, possessiveness and jealousy. Don't forget the idea of *ownership* which is associated with this planet. In some cases, a partner can be seen as a meal ticket or a status symbol. Pets can be loved to distraction but they are often also seen as possessions.

Like the Sun, Venus is associated with leisure and pleasure but there is a more sybaritic feel to this planet. An ordinary afternoon out in the Sun could merely involve a knockabout game of tennis, but an afternoon out in the company of Venus would mean soft music on the portable CD player and a sumptuous, boozy picnic, followed by a lazy love-making session among the flowers. The Venusian influence denotes relaxed enjoyment of all kinds with one's choice of pleasure depending upon one's mood and personality.

Subsidiary Definitions

Another connection between Venus and the Sun is that they are both associated with music. Venus is supposed to be especially concerned with singing, and I have found that many people who have a strong Venus in their charts either sing, play an instrument or dance, either as a hobby or as part of their work. People with Venus in Scorpio or Taurus have nice speaking voices. Like the Sun, Venus is associated with glamour and the nicer and more enjoyable aspects of life but the feeling is different. The Sun represents fun but Venus represents hedonism and luxury. An Indian lady once told me that her eleventh house Venus meant that she had many wealthy and influential friends and, although they were good for the occasional pleasant social outing, they did not help her to become rich or influential in her turn.

The position of Venus can give some clue as to whether or not the subject will ever have children. When activated by progression or transit, it can indicate birth, with female children being more likely than male ones. Be careful when dealing with anyone who wants children because you may get it wrong and give them false hopes. Better to be encouraging but a bit vague, I think.

All sorts of surprisingly deep emotions are wrapped up with this planet and some of these come under the rulership of other planets as well as Venus. For example, a secure home may be indicated by the Moon or Venus for slightly different reasons. Jealousy and possessiveness are shared between Venus, Pluto and, to some extent, Mars. Sentimentality, remembering an anniversary or valuing an object because of its history is definitely Venusian but these concepts can also apply to the Moon. Venus is definitely more materialistic than the Moon, and can be expressed as a need to hang on to what one has got, to covet another's goods or lifestyle, or to aspire to a better one for oneself.

Venus signifies relationships which are open and aboveboard and, therefore, is concerned with marriage-type partnerships, business partnerships and close associations of all kinds. It is also concerned with *open enemies* and therefore shows with whom we are likely to fight and why. In this respect, Venus is just as much a part of warfare as Mars. Nations go to war over territory or the right to trade, for tribal, historical or religious differences and for values and priorities which may not be shared or appreciated by the people they choose to fight.

Anything that appeals to the senses is ruled by Venus. This applies to cooking and eating, the smell of perfume, a beautiful garden or a lovely house, music, dancing, singing, art, culture, fashion or anything else which we enjoy. We all need a little elegance and refinement in our lives and Venus helps us to get it. Elegant and refined people have strong Venus influences on their charts. While writing this, my daughter asked if I fancied a smoked salmon sandwich for my lunch. My retrograde Venus, square to Saturn would have made just that — a smoked salmon sandwich — while Helen brought me a plate with a beautiful display of open sandwich, tomato, cucumber and lemon slices all lightly dredged in pepper. Helen has a very well-placed Venus in Libra! Astrology in action, what?

Obviously, Venus rules the feminine principle and is associated with all that is soft and feminine within every one of us but is, paradoxically, too materialistic to denote caring and sacrifice. This planet represents the beauty and sexual attractiveness of women. Imagine a young and lovely Victorian mother with a baby on her knee and an infant standing beside her. Who could resist her soft and gentle appeal? In those days, it would have taken a fair bit of money to guarantee the kind of easy lifestyle which would enable her to keep that beauty, and money is another Venusian consideration.

We all have a Venus on our charts and in a man's chart it can suggest the kind of woman who would attract him. For example, a man with Venus in a fire sign would want a pretty sparky type of mate, while one with Venus in a water sign would prefer a soft, slow, gentle and intuitive one.

Venus is also concerned with justice, balance and harmony and she will go openly into battle against an injustice if necessary.

This planet also has some connection to the law and lawyers although both Jupiter and Pluto are also associated with these.

MARS

> When the foeman bears his steel
> With uncomfortable zeal
> We find the wisest thing
> Is to slap our chests and sing
> Or when threatened with the mutes
> And our hearts are in our boots
> There is nothing brings it round
> Like the trumpet's martial sound
> Like the trumpet's martial sound.
>
> From *The Pirates of Penzance* by Gilbert and Sullivan

Mars rules Aries and, before the discovery of Pluto, it was also assigned to Scorpio. It rules the first house and was once also the ruler of the eighth house. Mars was, of course, the Roman god of war.

————————First Principles————————

Mars is associated with energy, force, drive, courage and the masculine side of all of us. A soldier needs a strong Mars. It is the macho aspect of the personality and, without Mars somewhere on our charts, nobody would never get up out of bed to do anything! A subject with a strong Mars on his chart is assertive, energetic and courageous. However, if the Mars energy is overdone, he or she could be hot-tempered, violent or self-destructive.

Mars denotes the kinds of activity which are often regarded as masculine rather than feminine, such as car maintenance, engineering, driving at speed and energetic sports. Team games, competitive sports and fighting are all very 'Martial'. Although not specifically associated with endurance, a good Mars in an earth sign would suggest the will and the strength to finish what one starts.

Whilst Venus can be exquisitely sensual and attractive in its soft and yielding beauty, Mars has the drive to make things happen. Mars, therefore, represents sexuality and the drive to perpetuate the human race. Aspects, transits and progressions to Mars can show times of intense sexual activity. Most of all Mars represents passion. This passion can be sexual, but it can also be expressed as love of this or hatred of that.

————————Subsidiary Definitions————————

Mars on a woman's chart can indicate the type of man she fancies. One very laid-back, gentle and rather slow-moving female friend of mine has a well-placed Mars in Scorpio and she is attracted to men in uniform and the Chippendales! Laughable as this may seem, her Mars attracts her to what she sees as 'real men' or 'he-men'.

Some women hand over the Mars side of their lives to their men, allowing them to make decisions for them or to 'look after' them. It is always worth taking a look to see what is happening to the Mars in a female client's chart, particularly if she is at the point of discovering that handing over the keys to her life to her man has turned out to be a mistake.

On a more practical level, Mars represents engineering and the kind of products on which mechanics and engineers work. Sharp objects such as knives, swords and anything else which is hard, 'macho' and durable is associated with Mars. Weapons and the means of firing projectiles and possibly the explosives themselves are Martian but there is a lot of cross-connection between Uranus which rules sudden explosions, earthquakes and, of course, uranium. Pluto rules plutonium, radiation, nuclear substances and their effects.

JUPITER

A more humane Mikado never did in Japan exist,
To nobody second, I'm certainly reckoned
A true philanthropist,
It is my very humane endeavour to make some extent,
Each evil liver a running river of harmless merriment.

From *The Mikado* by Gilbert and Sullivan

Jupiter is the first of the transpersonal planets and therefore less concerned with a subject's actions and feelings than with the way the subject experiences life in general. Jupiter (also called Jove), was the king of the Roman gods and, as such, could be very generous and philanthropic but also very angry and destructive to his subjects. Jupiter is associated with the sign of Sagittarius and the ninth house. Before the discovery of Neptune, Jupiter was also associated with the sign of Pisces and the twelfth house.

First Principles

Jupiter signifies expansion and exploration, thus anything which expands a subject's horizons. This planet has four very specific areas of rulership, these being higher education, religion or philosophy, the law, and overseas exploration. These subjects look, on the face of it, as if they have nothing in common with each other but when looked at from the point of view of *exploration and expansion*, they do.

Education expands the total quantity of a subject's knowledge and understanding. Mercury deals with the basic building blocks of literacy and numeracy, acquiring skills, gathering facts and accumulating knowledge. Jupiter is more concerned with the kind of higher education which makes a subject a more rounded person with a broader area of knowledge. While Mercury tries to pile in facts in order to get the subject through his school exams, Jupiter takes the time to think, to dream a little and to explore widely. Perhaps the difference is that Mercury increases knowledge while Jupiter increases understanding and, therefore, makes for a broader mind and a more tolerant attitude.

Nobody can become interested in a religion, philosophy or a particular manner of thinking unless he studies and thinks about it. A subject's philosophy or religious beliefs are a personal matter which he must come to over a period of time and with a certain amount of living under his belt. Depth of knowledge and understanding characterise both these ideas. Unfortunately, certain religious beliefs can decrease knowledge and understanding and, instead of bringing enlightenment, engender fear, hatred and intolerance of anything which is different. This darker side of the old Roman god's nature surfaces all too often here.

The law is much more specific in that one must consult a specialist in order to deal with it. In the past solicitors administered land, inheritances and money matters and to some extent, they still do, but the complications of taxation and the modern business world mean that accountancy has now become a separate field. To be honest, I see no reason why the *expertise* which is involved here shouldn't be considered a Jupiterian matter, even though the specific career of banking is traditionally assigned to Capricorn.

The law may not seem to have much to do with exploration, etc. but it does have a good deal to do with boundaries. Test cases explore the boundaries of mankind's behaviour and new laws are needed whenever a situation gets out of hand. People continually test the law to see just where the boundaries lie. The law can be used to protect the population or to repress it, a fact that illustrates the dark side of Jove once again!

The notion of exploration and expansion in connection with foreign travel is obvious, but I wonder now where we draw the line. Mass travel is such a modern concept that astrology hasn't yet caught up with it, so perhaps now is the time to do so. Perhaps regular journeys to an overseas holiday home or to a business destination could perhaps be considered Mercurial. After all, there is little to explore or to expand a subject's horizons in this kind of scenario. Visiting strange new lands, even in the comfort of an air-conditioned coach, *could* be deemed exploration, so perhaps these belong to Jupiter. As in the chapter on Mercury, I shall leave it to each individual astrologer to work it out. Travel broadens the mind (although it lightens the wallet), so it adds to one's level of knowledge and understanding.

Subsidiary Definitions

Newspaper and magazine astrological columnists like myself use Jupiter to signal times of opportunity and luck, especially in connection with money. In deeper predictive astrology, an aspect from Jupiter to another planet can bring losses, although these, ultimately, force changes for the better. This planet also brings chance meetings with important new people, and many other things which tend to lead to improved circumstances of all kinds. Jupiter is a 'lucky planet' in many ways but we must remember that the old Roman god threw thunderbolts as well as bouquets, so the luck can come in very funny ways. The best attitude to take is that Jupiter creates a window of opportunity as long as one is wise, courageous or desperate enough to open it and clamber through it. Jupiter is associated with financial and business opportunities, especially if they bring expansion, growth and greater depth to an enterprise. A transit from Jupiter may actually bring losses but these could be followed by changes of direction which are ultimately beneficial.

Jupiter is associated with publishing and, nowadays, also with broadcasting. This, like so much else that Jupiter deals with, seems to be related to Mercury, for although the act of thinking and writing are Mercurial, the aim of publishing and broadcasting is to ensure that the writer's ideas reach as wide a public as possible, and activity on this scale is more appropriate to Jupiter.

Jupiter is a tolerant and broadminded planet and people who have Jupiterian charts are racially tolerant, even to the point of actually seeking out people of a different cultural background for friends, colleagues and marriage partners. Such people hate and abhor racial or religious intolerance and will do much to protect minorities.

Through its association with Pisces, Jupiter can be associated with the caring professions. Jupiterian people understand the need for all of us to care for each other and to be part of the world we live in, rather than simply to take what we want at the expense of others. The modern concept of ecology and the desire to save the planet, to preserve the forests, seas and animals is very Jupiterian. It is the sense of the wholeness and oneness of the world, and of matters which go beyond the boundaries of each of our own lives which is important here.

Jupiter is associated with generosity, glamour, 'glitz' and the desire to live life to the full. Jupiterian people have expanded horizons, wonderful lifestyles, expanded waistlines and big hearts. Jupiter vies with the Sun in its desire for greatness, material and spiritual success and a worthwhile lifestyle.

Jupiter is supposed to rule large animals and the outdoor life. I am no expert on mythology but I seem to remember a story about Jupiter disguising himself as a bull in order to carry off the beautiful and fanciable Europa. Perhaps it is this myth which connects Jupiter to large animals!

Jupiterian concepts include sports and competitive activities although in the sense of competition for the fun of it rather than serious dedication. Mars rules the Olympics while Jupiter rules 'It's a Knockout'! Enjoyment of the countryside, animals, sporting activities and an 'eat, drink and be merry' attitude are very Jupiterian. Gambling, especially horse racing and *winning* are associated with this lucky planet.

Jupiterian people are extremely humorous. Some actually make a living as comedians. The Jupiterian humour is rarely subtle, but silly and rather schoolboyish.

SATURN

To sit in solemn silence in a dull, dark dock,
In a pestilential prison with a life long lock,
Awaiting the sensation of a short sharp shock,
From a cheeky chippy on a big black block!

From *The Mikado* by Gilbert and Sullivan

Saturn is the other transpersonal planet and therefore it is less concerned with a subject's actions than the way he experiences life itself. Saturn rules Capricorn and the tenth house. Before Uranus was discovered, Saturn also ruled Aquarius and the eleventh house. Saturn was the Roman god of time and the ruler of old age.

Beginners in astrology love to hate poor old Saturn and they rush to blame it for all their problems. There is nothing *wrong* with Saturn as long as one accepts that into each life a little rain must fall! Saturn ensures that we get down to work and don't waste our lives loafing around. It also allows a contrast between good times and bad, so that we learn to appreciate the good things when they come along.

First Principles

Saturn does rule a few material *things*, in the same way that the previous six planets do, but it seems to be far more concerned with the *concepts* of practicality, organisational skills and self-discipline. Without Saturn, it would be impossible to get anything done. Saturn sets boundaries, sometimes the same ones that Jupiter is trying to push away, sometimes different ones. The word most often used in connection with this planet is *limitation*, because Saturn shows where and how we are limited by circumstances. Another typical explanation is that Saturn is the *teacher of the zodiac* who makes us work hard to achieve our goals. Saturn should not be considered as being the enemy within, but the means of learning and developing and of giving us the character and backbone that we need in order to get through life.

A 'difficult' Saturn *can* bring severe limitations in health or physical ability, or it may block the mental faculties and the ability to live a full life. You may remember that in the chapter on Mercury, I mentioned an ex-neighbour of mine who had a mentally handicapped daughter. This youngster's Mercury was conjunct Saturn, in Scorpio, in the twelfth house. This is a particularly difficult combination to overcome, but the girl grew up in a loving environment and she developed as far as she could under the circumstances. The key word here is *circumstances* and that, to me, is the key to Saturn.

We all live with some kind of limitation at some time in our lives. Some of us are born into difficult circumstances, others find them along the way. My wise old grandma had a saying which, roughly translated from Yiddish, said: 'Everyone gets their share of aggravation in life, be it early or late, everyone gets their share!' Sometimes it is hard to see that any aggravation exists in the lives of some people, but nothing is what it seems. While we are busy envying our neighbour, we are unaware of what they have experienced in the past, what goes on behind closed doors, or what is to follow.

Saturn also rules structure. A house must be built on firm foundations or it will collapse at the first hint of bad weather. If one takes the comparison between buying oneself a high fashion bargain outfit which has a short and happy life, or an expensive, good quality outfit which will look good for many years, the choice of the good quality item would be a Saturnian one. Work which is carried out in an orderly, structured and disciplined manner is Saturnian. A quiet and well-behaved child who is conscientious about his homework and his household chores is Saturnian — (possibly far *too* Saturnian to be mentally healthy). Anything which is done thoroughly and properly is Saturnian; thus, this planet rules craftsmanship, attention to detail and the art of finishing what one starts.

Saturn is connected to responsibilities and obligations, the need to put other considerations before oneself. We tend to respect the type of person who does this and to despise the one who walks away from responsibilities or refuses to put himself out to help others. Too much Saturn can result in a subject being *controlled* or *dictated to* by others. He may cope with this situation by enduring it, because endurance is another Saturnian concept.

Just as the Moon rules a subject's experience of being nurtured, Saturn shows how he was disciplined. A well-placed Saturn, along with other happy childhood features on a chart, would denote that a child experienced teaching by encouragement and saw discipline as a form of security. Parents, teachers and other guardians *cared*, and set sensible limitations such as regular meals, a reasonable bedtime, homework, school attendance, etc. Such concepts as team games, joint efforts and the family pulling together in order to achieve something worthwhile are all Saturnian.

As far as material concepts are concerned, Saturn rules banking, big business, large structures and organisations, and probably the earth itself. Serious matters and serious people are Saturnian. Saturn rules the metal lead, and by extension, rules radiation shields. It also rules heaviness in all its forms ranging from a heavy object to a heavy heart!

Subsidiary Definitions

Saturn is often depicted as 'Old Father Time' and is considered to be the ruler of old age. Human beings tend to want everything that is good in life *right now* and find it hard to wait for good times to come along. We understand the concept of planting something and then waiting for it to grow, but when nothing exciting or interesting is happening in our own lives we complain that we are 'in limbo'. Clients often visit astrologers and other consultants when they feel that they are in this state, in order to find out when things are going to change. Some even prefer bad times to those when nothing at all is going on. Saturn's journey through a particular sign or house can mean that nothing much happens in that area of life for a while.

There is a beneficial side to Saturn and a lighter side too. The benefits of Saturn are rewards from hard work and the results gained from seeing projects through to the end. The tortoise in the old fable of the tortoise and the hare shows how it is done. (I have always had a sneaking regard for the hare because he also gets there too in the end, but he sees and does so many more interesting things along the way!) Saturn brings the sense of achievement which comes from passing exams, getting through the driving test, getting a book written and published (not half!) or getting a well-deserved promotion, being given a bonus or doing a pile of ironing! The tangible results are a well-deserved feeling of success, increased status, more money, an organised kitchen, royalty payments, or a myriad other well-earned blessings.

Getting older is good for many people. In many other countries, the inhabitants would love the chance to live to see old age and, better still, to be able to enjoy it in good health and with good food on the table. In the developed world, senior citizenship can be a very happy time. The struggles and responsibilities of youth have passed and, if one is lucky, the children are glad to return the love and help which they themselves received when young. There is time and the money for hobbies and interests. Saturn is the road to the sea, the last part of a long trip across a hard land.

However, there are some really unpleasant concepts which come under the realm of Saturn. For example, intense, crippling shyness, self-doubt, low self-esteem, self-hatred, severe embarrassment, a blow to the ego, and also suffering and loss of many kinds. But, before you slide back into the habit of blaming Saturn for every ill, please remember that all the planets have a down-side. To take the two most beneficial and benign planets in the system as examples, Venusian jealousy and greed can lead to enormous suffering, Jupiterian dogma and the intense need to escape from reality can lead to different kinds of heartache. Before Pluto was discovered, Saturn was considered to be the most 'malefic' planet and, as such, associated with death.

URANUS

On better far to live and die
Under the brave black flag I fly,
Than play a sanctimonious part
With a pirate head and a pirate heart,
For across the world and over the sea,
The pirates all have law degrees,
But I'll remain true to the song that I sing,
And live and die a pirate king!

From *The Pirates of Penzance* by Gilbert and Sullivan

Uranus rules Aquarius and the eleventh house. Before Uranus was discovered, these were ruled by Saturn. The mythology of Uranus does not tie up terribly well with astrology except, perhaps, for the idea of rebellion and refusal to conform. Uranus was the god of the stormy heavens and the son of Gaia, the Earth goddess. He was castrated by Saturn who, immediately afterwards, threw Uranus's genitals into the sea. The foaming stormy mess of blood and semen bubbled and bubbled and eventually gave birth to Venus. (After all this activity, Uranus retired from his godly duties and moved to Worthing to play bowls!!!)

————————History————————

Uranus is the first of the impersonal planets, also referred to as the outer planets. These planets take several years to move through each sign and therefore represent a particular era, a period of time and the thinking that goes along with it. These are the planets of zeitgeist (the spirit of a particular time).

The planet Uranus was discovered in 1871 by William Herschel. In England, the industrial revolution was underway and the changes which it was to bring were beginning to be felt. Over the next century or so, the population grew, cities spread, and a greater understanding of public health erased the widespread mortality caused by the pandemic plagues of previous times. Agriculture allowed the population to be fed rather than allowing small groups to subsist. A middle class emerged, ordinary people began to reach for a better way of life, intellectualism increased and education gradually became universal. The old power groups of absolute monarchies, aristocrats, robber barons and large landowners began to break up for the first time in history, and experiments in other means of public organisation began to emerge. Chartists, communards, socialists, Marxists, fascists and Bolsheviks began to have their day. The cry was for freedom from tyranny but, ironically, these Uranian ideas sometimes created an even greater tyranny in their turn. The inventions of the past two hundred years have brought more advances than occurred in the whole of the previous history of man.

────────First Principles────────

My friend, Denise, calls Uranus the 'breakout' planet. Years ago, when I was learning about astrology, much was made of the totalitarian nature of Uranus. This planet was seen as the one which caused revolutions, changed the old order and put something in its place that is run by a committee. Uranian ideas were said to be idealistic and utilitarian, devoted to equality and to the submerging of individual feelings, desires and needs. It's funny how ideas change even within the space of half a lifetime. Uranus is now seen as being associated with quirky individualism and a desire for freedom and independence. Uranus rules idealism, humanitarianism and many other isms. The family unit and individual needs are supposed to be seen as less important than the needs of the community. In the time of the hippies, who were devoted to the rise of the Aquarian age, communal living was all the rage. Yet, in reality, Uranian people live first and foremost for themselves and they don't take account of the opinions of others.

Groups and group activities are specifically Uranian. Typical examples would be organisations devoted to 'green' issues, trade unions, societies and community centres geared to the needs of the poor, the deprived or to cultural minorities. Looking around the friends whom I have made through group activities of this kind, this is what I find. Astrological organisations are filled with Aquarians and Sagittarians when they start out, but these begin to drift away once the ideas have been floated and the details need to be dealt with. Non-astrological groups seem to attract a variety of Sun signs, with Aries and Cancer being fairly close to the top of the list.

Uranus rules friendship and acquaintanceship rather than close personal relationships, and Uranian people do have many friends as well as being more or less close to their families. However, this planet values its freedom and finds clinging, possessive or demanding people abhorrent. Uranus is concerned with the need to learn for oneself, to find out the hard way and to do it alone and without help whenever possible.

Uranus is associated with education in all its forms and, like

Jupiter and Mercury, it wants to see ideas and knowledge being spread as far and as widely as possible. The connection to ideas and logic can make it seem a bit cold and unfeeling at times. Mr Spock would have approved.

This modern planet is associated with nineteenth-century inventions such as electricity and the discovery of radiation, Radium and Uranium. It is also connected to twentieth-century developments such as radar, computers, television and satellites. Improvements in transport, flight and space technology are all Uranian concepts. Some of these concepts cross over into the realms of Mercury but the idea of modern devices and the very widespread dissemination of information is Uranian.

————————Subsidiary Definitions————————

Uranus signifies obstinacy and the kind of bloody-minded determination that gets things done. It denotes eccentricity and individuality and it is true that strongly Uranian people do live in a completely individual way. Some choose to work with large groups of people but live alone, or to live with large groups of people in a kind of commune but work alone. Others live and work alone but their work reaches many thousands of people though the media or through publishing of one kind or another.

Although Jupiter is the traditional planet associated with publishing, I think that Uranus fits the bill too with its need to spread new ideas. Newsletters seem to be a favourite Uranian medium. I have three lying about on my desk at the moment, all produced by Aquarians. One is on computers, the second on astrology and psychic matters and the third on witchcraft.

Uranus breaks down barriers and, like the Tower in a pack of Tarot cards, often destroys something which has been around for too long. This destruction allows light to filter in through the wreckage and this offers the people concerned the opportunity to see and understand the truth of the matter. Therefore, revelation and change are very Uranian.

Unusual people or unusual responses to anything are Uranian, as are flashes of genius, intuition, clairvoyance, sudden shocks, and life-changing events. So are visitations from the other side, science fact and science fiction and the kind of imagination which produces both of these, and almost anything else which is weird and different.

NEPTUNE

We must dance and we must sing
All around our fairy ring
We indulge in all our dancing
In a fashion most entrancing
If you ask what special function
Sets our miracles in motion
We reply without compunction
That we haven't any notion.

From *Iolanthe* by Gilbert and Sullivan

Neptune rules Pisces and the twelfth house. Before Neptune was discovered, this sign and house were ruled by Jupiter. In mythology, Neptune was the god of the sea and the earthshaker who is supposed to have caused earthquakes. There is not much to tie Neptune to astrology except for the odd fact that the two Moons of Neptune are called Oberon and Titania. These two were the god and goddess of dreams in addition to being the King and Queen of the fairies, which Shakespeare used in his play, *A Midsummer Night's Dream*.

History

Neptune was discovered by John Adams and Urbain LeVerrier in 1846. My schoolgirl French suggests that LeVerrier may mean glass-maker. It is an interesting thought that glass is so clear that it *disappears*, it is equally interesting to note than Neptune also rules glass. Glass is so good at giving the illusion of not being there that I have had to stick a pretty design on the glass door between the two parts of my office to prevent me from walking into it!

Neptune doesn't seem to be as closely involved with historical changes as Uranus, or even Pluto, probably because it is not *political* in nature. However, it was discovered at a time when coal and gas became common energy sources for both lighting and heating, and this contributed to the increased wealth of the nation (if not to all of its inhabitants) by allowing factories to operate by day and by night.

Historically, Neptune seems to have come into its own in the 1960s and 1970s when the flower-power people were around. This period brought the idea of collective responsibility of a particularly gentle kind, but all this was against a backdrop of a strange and devastating war. In 1846 there was no chemical industry, no organised and *industrial* pharmaceutical industry and no anaesthetics. Drugs are a boon which have made life possible and comfortable for many millions – just consider the plight of a diabetic in 1846. Drug misuse has become widespread since the sixties, while the cost of legitimate medical drugs is skyrocketing. Perhaps we will soon be back to brewing up something in our own cauldrons. In the 19th century the Salvation Army did much to reduce the devastating effects of drink by means of a combination of social work and religion, but there are still people who abuse this ordinary pleasure, and prohibition only served to make a few gangsters very rich. Everything about Neptune is contradictory and confusing, filled with the very best of man's aspirations and the very worst of his degrading excesses.

First Principles

Neptune rules concepts which are hard to describe such as inspiration, imagination, illusion and delusion. This planet rules the appreciation of things which are beyond the basic needs of food, clothing and shelter. Neptune presides over artistry, music and the kind of illusion created by film, television and evocative music. There are a number of 'creative' planets but Neptune brings creativity to life and allows us to laugh or cry over the antics of a cartoon character or become totally absorbed by whatever we are watching, hearing, sensing and enjoying. Film and television are especially Neptunian because, not only are these imaginary and illusory, but they are also showing pictures of actors and players who are, by the time we see them, *no longer there*!

Neptune brings truth, light and god-given wisdom but it also muddles and confuses and causes us to lose our way. This planet is associated with kindness, pity, charity and love but these concepts can all too easily be twisted and misused. Many ordinary people have given freely to the starving people in Somalia, Ethiopia and the Sudan only to discover that the goods they have bought have been hi-jacked and the aid organisations made to pay for safe passage.

Mysticism, religious inspiration and a life dedicated to the work of whatever God we believe in are all very Neptunian, but so is fanaticism and religious intolerance. Neptune signifies love, and this can be the purest love of God, the love of one's children or of one's fellow man, but it also rules falling in love. When someone falls in love, he is confused, unable to think straight and he may even be unable to eat, sleep and function normally for a while. Unrequited love is particularly Neptunian, as is the kind of love which blinds a subject to the truth.

Mystical psychic experiences are Neptunian but delving into the occult is probably more attributable to Pluto. Neptune deals with things that we cannot see clearly, but Pluto deals with things that we cannot see at all!

Neptune denotes escape from the world, confinement by choice, or otherwise, and disappearing acts of one kind or another. Therefore, the rulership of Neptune includes orphanages, asylums, hospitals, prisons and hospices or any other place where people are confined either for their own good or for the good of society. This planet is also connected to religious retreats, enclosed orders and any other means of escape or of retreat from the world. Drink and drugs are a means of escape for some people, while going over the wall at Colditz or walking away from a marriage by going out to buy a packet of cigarettes and disappearing, are others. A holiday is a short-term means of escape for most of us and as many holidays are taken by or on water (even skiing) this is all very Neptunian in character.

Deceptions, lies and confidence tricks are Neptunian, as are muddles, mistakes and things that go missing in the post (although this can also be a Mercury problem). Neptune can mess up almost anything and make it seem to be something other than what it is. If a business, an enterprise or an organisation is born with Neptune on the ascendant, descendant or in the seventh house, there will always be muddles, losses and confusion. Neptune wouldn't be very good in the tenth house either, and would only suit an enterprise that was Neptunian in concept.

This planet is associated with the sea, fish and fishing. The connections with Jesus Christ and the disciples is very strong and the first symbol of Christianity, long before the cross, was the sign of the fish. This period of history coincided with the great age of Pisces, and Pisces, of course, is ruled by Neptune.

Idealists, masochists, visionaries and 'nutters' all come under the cloak of Neptune!

Subsidiary Definitions

Neptune rules the unconscious and, therefore, a transit from this planet can unlock things from a subject's past.

Hypnotherapy is Neptunian because it unlocks the memory and also because it causes an altered state of consciousness. Great happiness and joy are Neptunian, as is the confusion of emotions when one loses something or someone important. Seeing life or seeing another person through rose-coloured glasses or imagining insults or misunderstanding motives are also Neptunian.

Neptunian jobs include working in hospitals, mental institutions and prisons. Charity work — with or without religious connections — is also Neptunian.

PLUTO

Behold the Lord High Executioner,
A personage of noble rank and title,
A dignified and potent officer,
Whose functions are particularly vital!

From *The Mikado* by Gilbert and Sullivan

Pluto rules Scorpio and the eighth house. Before the discovery of Pluto, Scorpio was ruled by Mars. It is the last of our planets and is, of course, another impersonal one. In Roman mythology, Pluto was the king of the underworld. There was also a god known as Plutus, who was the god of wealth.

You may remember reading the story of Orpheus and Euridice. Pluto, a great womaniser, took a fancy to Euridice and took her to live with him in the underworld. Orpheus, her lover, was distraught and he tried to get her back. He asked Mercury to negotiate her release but unusually for him, Mercury had no luck. So Orpheus picked up his lyre and charmed Charon the boatman into taking him across the Styx, then he charmed Cerberus the three-headed dog into letting him into Hades. Eventually he got to Pluto and used his songs and music to try to charm him. Pluto was unmoved and declared himself to be 'reality, the unresponsive audience'. Euridice prayed to Pluto and eventually he relented. Orpheus was told to lead her out of the underworld, a three-day journey, and while doing so, not to look back or check that she was behind him, or he would lose her. At some point on the last day, Orpheus couldn't be sure that Euridice was following, so he took a peek behind him. She *was* there but, to his horror, she suddenly began to recede back into the underworld. Orpheus was devastated and not much helped by a message from Pluto that death is always stronger than love or trust.

There are many people who have had the experience of losing a loved one and then dreaming that they were chasing them down a dark tunnel or across a dark river, only to see them accelerate away from them. I had this experience myself when I was only eight years old. Perhaps these common human experiences are where the mythology of the underworld originated from.

History

Pluto was discovered in 1930 by Sir Percival Lowell. When I was learning astrology, much was made of the discovery of Pluto heralding the age of nuclear destruction. Radium had already been discovered but the use of nuclear fusion and fission were only developed during the Second World War.

1930 was a time of delicate and precarious balance in Europe. The currency inflation of the Weimar Republic was at an end and there was a good relationship between the French and German Foreign Ministers, Stresemann and Briand. This, however, was not to last and the rise of Hitler and the coming of the Second World War brought the nuclear age into being.

Pluto's journey through Scorpio has brought the end of the Soviet Empire and the rise of AIDS. Pluto will be entering Sagittarius in 1995 and this will bring massive changes of yet another kind. But what? We can only speculate.

──────────────**First Principles**──────────────

Pluto rules the deeper and more difficult aspects of our lives and it is the planet associated with death. Spiritual people see the death of a person as a means of passing from one state to another, often leading to the beginning of another incarnation in another lifetime. Pluto signifies mourning, loss, the pain of rejection, partings and complete endings of long-term situations.

In all forms of divination, whether by astrology, Tarot or any other means, death is most considered to be the end of *something* rather than the death of a human being and, therefore, is seen as a form of transformation. This planet suggests that everything must change and be recycled. I've seen people get married on a Pluto transit, move house or in some other way, change their lives completely from one condition to another. Pluto always brings beginnings as well as endings and it links the two. When a child leaves home, this is an ending but it is also a beginning.

The theme of recycling is a popular one nowadays and the idea of saving something and re-using it in a different form is a very Plutonian one. The idea of saving money, stopping wastefulness and saving the planet all adds to our collective wealth and, therefore, is allied to Plutonian riches and plenty.

Venus may rule our personal finances but Pluto presides over joint finances and other people's money. A subject's lifestyle will change if his/her partner's fortunes either increase or decrease, if a parent suddenly becomes rich or loses all his wealth or when children become independent. If an employee's firm goes bust, the employee loses his income; if the firm does well, he might be promoted to a better position with a better salary. Our fortunes are often affected by circumstances which surround us but which are not of our own making.

Pluto is associated with wills, legacies and corporate matters. It may not rule business as such, but the act of becoming involved in a business or changes which occur within that business are definitely involved. Pluto rules tax bills and the tax man, also the stock market and shares of all kinds. I would think that pensions and insurance, especially life insurance, come under this planet, while the administration of other people's finances definitely does.

Pluto rules procreation as well as death, both in the sense of bringing a new life into the world as well as the birth of an enterprise or an idea. A new start, a new way of life and a complete change of outlook can be influenced by Pluto. Except in a few cases where artificial insemination or out-of-the-body fertilisation are concerned, most births come about as a result of two people making love; therefore, sex is also ruled by Pluto. Pluto was a very sexy god who took the best and the most beautiful women for himself whenever he could. Pluto presides over sexual scandals, prostitution (with some help from Venus) and sexual indiscretions. Pluto is also concerned with committed relationships and long-term joint arrangements which involve sex, money or both.

——————Subsidiary Definitions——————

Pluto presides over all that is hidden, especially anything that is under the ground or is very valuable. This includes the mining of gold, diamonds, coal and anything else which has to be dug up. Bank vaults are especially Plutonic, as is archaeology.

Some health problems are Plutonic. Anything which involves the genitals or reproductive organs is obviously Plutonic, but the idea of something going wrong inside where it cannot be seen also fits the picture. Surgery is definitely Plutonic because it cuts through to what is inside. Knives and the use of them for good and ill are ruled by Pluto (and Mars). Pluto is concerned with butchery, both in the sense of killing animals for food and also cutting them up. Engineering and mechanical skills are also Pluto ruled.

Due to Pluto's association with the covert, it is associated with investigations of all kinds. For example, the police, Interpol, forensic science, espionage and counter-intelligence. Some mystery and thriller writers have a particularly Plutonic outlook. Military matters are somewhat involved with Pluto, in addition to Mars and Venus (Venus rules open enemies). Such concepts as unarmed combat and karate are Plutonic, especially when they result in death!

Pluto signifies power games and manipulative behaviour and Plutonic people often enjoy being the power behind the throne rather than the obvious leader. These people don't like to show themselves off in an open and obvious manner and they appear to have no vanity. However, they are very proud, even if their achievements are not outwardly obvious. Plutonic people can also be king-makers or the kind of parent who pushes his children into becoming very successful.

Psychiatry is ruled by Pluto and this is quite obvious when one considers it. Hypnotherapy is both Neptunian and Plutonian in nature, as is anything else which gets to the bottom of an obsession, a blockage or a socio-sexual problem. Family hatreds over money matters and business disagreements which bring intense feelings are Plutonic. Deep and abiding love are also Plutonic but this too can be very destructive if wrongly directed.

Pluto is concerned with the unconscious, both on a personal level of unconscious motives or of a hidden agenda, but also on a group level. The zeitgeist, or spirit of a particular time, is Plutonic (although this also applies to the nodes of the Moon). This planet offers opportunities for change, inner improvement and the changing of other people's outlook, either singly or in large groups.

Pluto is far from being all bad. Everything has to be recycled if life is to be sustained and the saving of waste and the recycling of products is an excellent idea. Love, birth and the righting of wrongs are not evil and neither is the discovery of that which is hidden or lost. Sometimes power needs to be wielded in a subtle and covert manner and not everything should be open to scrutiny. Surgery heals, butchery feeds. Farm animals and mining sustain nations. Wealth must be created jointly and shared among others. Wills, legacies, taxes and corporate matters sustain civilisation. Without sex, none of us would be here. This may be a difficult area to cope with in an astrological reading but it is important.

CHIRON

Chiron is not a planet at all, but an asteroid. It is being given attention by a great many astrologers these days, probably due to the fact that its position is now recorded in various ephemerides. Chiron is known as the wounded healer and the 'planet' is said to be concerned with physical and emotional pain. If you want to look up the position of Chiron you will either need a computer program which gives this or a copy of the *American Ephemeris for the 20th Century* by Neil F. Michelsen.

If you enjoy mythology and if it helps to understand the symbolism of the planets, this should help you. The information for this has been supplied by my mythology expert, Jonathan Dee. Any misspellings or errors in this section are entirely mine.

Chiron was the king of the centaurs and the teacher of heroes, including Hercules, Jason and Perseus. He was accidentally shot in the heel by one of Hercules' poisoned arrows and the wound festered. Chiron couldn't be cured but, being immortal, he couldn't die either, so he suffered terribly.

Meanwhile, Prometheus (this is the Greek name for the Roman god Uranus) was tied to a rock in the sea while his liver was pecked at by birds. Hercules freed Prometheus. Prometheus had lost his immortality, and when he asked Zeus to give it back, Zeus couldn't help him, unless he found someone to swap it with. Chiron happily agreed to this so that he could give up his suffering and die, going on to take a place in the heavens as the constellation Centaurus.

It interesting to note that, before his accident, Chiron was known as the greatest of the healers. His daughter, Manta, was said to have invented astrology and it is her name which is given to the 'mantic arts', e.g. chiromancy, crystalmancy, etc.

A strong Chiron in a birthchart encourages a subject to work in medicine, teaching or counselling, possibly because this person knows what it is like to need help.

I have had a quick look at the position of Chiron in the charts of the people around me and it seems to have the greatest influence when it is close to the angles or in angular houses. This follows Michel Gauquelin's findings that planets have the strongest influence when close to the angles, particularly the ascendant or midheaven. Try looking at people with Chiron close to the midheaven or nadir for difficult relationships with parents, or close to the ascendant or descendant for personal problems or difficulties in sexual relationships. As you can see, this is all in the early stages of research. Many astrologers associate Chiron with Sagittarius, but others (including myself) see Virgo as being much more relevant.

CHAPTER 6

The Planets Through the Signs

SUN SIGNS

It is extremely tricky to treat the Sun in the same way that one does all the other planets because it doesn't have the same kind of practical applications. Nevertheless, in the first segment of each Sun sign, I have chosen to pick out just one of the Sun's areas of involvement, (creativity, children, achievements, amusements, etc.), assessing how this might be expressed. To take a silly example; what kind of gold and jewellery would different Sun signs buy themselves? Would a Taurean buy Krugerrands? Would a Piscean buy Jade or a piece of rock-crystal set on a silver pendant? Would a Gemini choose earrings or two matching bracelets?

The second part of each Sun sign slides into the usual kind of pop-astrology Sun-sign explanation. This may be an inelegant way to approach the Sun in astrology, but I am trying to make these subtle and nebulous ideas as concrete as I can and as easy as possible for student astrologers to grasp.

I suggest that, if you are a beginner, you read all the Sun sign books you can get your hands on, including both the populist ones and the deeper, more psychologically-based ones. Concentrate on those signs in which you are *least* interested as well as your own or those of your nearest and dearest.

—How The Sun Expresses Itself in Aries—

This is a masculine fire sign which is cardinal in nature. Ariens are energetic, enterprising, outgoing and competitive. The Sun's own energies, therefore, are expressed in an adventurous, impulsive, competitive, 'I-want-it-now!' manner. An example might be of the subject's attitude to his children. This attitude would be extremely competitive: he would see his own children as being an extension of himself and he would want them to be winners, high-achievers and a shining advert for his success as a parent.

Sun in Aries People

A typical Arien won't let the grass grow under his feet but he is impatient with details, easily bored and needs to be busy both at work and socially. Ariens like to be part of a large organisation with a set structure and a ladder to climb. If they work for themselves, they will find a way of joining up with others or of leading a team. Somewhat impulsive and always optimistic, Ariens look forward with faith in the future and they don't usually bear grudges. These subjects are kind hearted and very good to their friends and family, they are generous and helpful and very good hosts or hostesses.

Ariens are competitive and they like to be the best of the bunch, but they make poor salespersons. This is partly due to the fact that they are surprisingly shy and also that they lack the persistence which is needed for sales work. Aries women need a career outside the home, and both men and women often have hobbies in addition to demanding careers. These subjects cannot sit about for long and they are not great television viewers because they are restless and easily bored. They make loving parents although they may push their children too hard, but they will do anything they can to help them. Ariens are surprisingly home-loving and, while some enjoy roaming the world, most are not actually keen on travel.

Most appreciate art or beauty but they may be too impatient to do anything artistic themselves. These subjects have an excellent sense of humour. Ariens have a surprisingly spiritual side to them which attracts them to a particular kind of religion or a spiritual way of thinking. A surprising number of them are drawn to mediumism and their intuition and keen interest in spiritual life can make them excellent clairvoyants and psychometrists.

—How The Sun Expresses Itself in Taurus—

This is a feminine earth sign which is fixed in nature. Taurcans are practical, patient, thorough, tenacious and reliable. The Sun in Taurus acts in a slow and patient manner, with thought and a common-sense attitude. Anything which is ruled by the Sun is expressed in a creative manner and it should bring in a concrete result. The road to success and achievement would be through something solidly creative, such as building or landscape gardening, and the best thing to come out of any enterprise would be wealth, either in place of, or alongside, excitement or glamour.

Sun in Taurus People

The Taurean's chief fault is stubbornness and an unwillingness to make changes. The fixed/earth combination makes them very hard to shift. Traditionally, Taureans are considered to be interested in food and money and, while they may have many other interests, these former matters are never too far from their thoughts. Taureans need to feel secure and to have a well-filled bank account behind them. These subjects are close to their families and very loyal to their friends, but they make implacable enemies. They may irritate their partners or their children by wanting to know exactly where they are going and what time they are coming home.

These dexterous people often find work in artistic or creative fields and many of them make inspired builders or decorators. Many Taureans enjoy gardening, cooking, music or working with make-up. Most of all, they love to be on holiday with their family and friends, having a nice time strolling around in the sunshine. They are usually pleasant, ordinary and very reliable. There is a breed of Taurean man who becomes impossible to live with as he gets older. This man is only interested in money, sprawling in front of the telly and grumbling. Fortunately, most Taureans are not like this at all. Taureans can miss the boat in matters of work or relationships because they tend to wait too long before making a move. Another peculiarity is that they tend not to show outsiders their best side which means that they are often taken for fools.

These subjects are not fools, for they often have a great depth of knowledge and wisdom which, for some reason, is often hidden. Taurean behaviour is often a cover for shyness and the kind of deep feelings which they prefer to keep hidden.

—How the Sun Expresses Itself in Gemini—

Gemini is a masculine air sign which is mutable in nature, therefore it is changeable and intellectual in its approach. The Sun in Gemini expresses itself by absorbing information and releasing it again. Therefore, we will take one Solar attribute as an illustration: a love affair, for example, would include as much chat and laughter as sex.

Sun in Gemini People

Geminis *can* live and work alone but they draw people to them and their phone is rarely at rest. Gemini subjects are astute and often quite intellectual but they may hop from one subject to another without studying anything too deeply. However, if their interest is aroused, they can go into something to a greater depth. Boredom is their worst enemy. These subjects are loyal to their families and friends and they don't like too many changes in their relationships but, like all air signs, they can drift in and out of friendships as the mood takes them. These excellent communicators often work in jobs which keep them in touch with others and many of them work in the media. Many Geminis are attracted to figure work and, although this is not common astrological knowledge, a great many Geminis work in banking and accountancy. So much for their inability to concentrate on details!

Geminis enjoy travel and sports but they are not outdoorsy or strong. They need to rest as much as they can and conserve their easily-depleted physical energies. These subjects are more sensible and hard working than they are given credit for, and they are quite determined to climb the career ladder. Gemini women often marry domestic men who are better at cooking and housekeeping than they are. Geminis need personal freedom and hate being questioned about their comings and goings. Some Geminis are very self-involved and can whine when things go wrong, while others simply make the best of things and get on with it. However, most of them are very nervous with a tendency to worry about nothing, while some can be real pessimists.

—How the Sun Expresses Itself in Cancer—

Cancer is a feminine water sign which is cardinal in nature. Cardinal signs like to make their own decisions and the water element brings in a lot of feeling, intuition and sensitivity, but it also brings restlessness and rather overwhelming emotions. If we want to take one aspect of the Sun's character and see how it works through Cancer, we could look at business matters. In this case, any business would be conducted on a very personal basis and it would include buying, selling and dealing with the public.

Sun in Cancer People

Cancerians are sensitive and easily hurt but they learn to hide their sensitivity under a hard shell and, in some cases over a period of time, the soft heart atrophies leaving nothing but the shell. Cancerians do well in caring professions and dealing with the public on a business basis. They have an instinctive feel for what people need, and they provide this with charm and efficiency. They can calm those who are angry or even hysterical without becoming infected with anger themselves, providing this situation occurs in a *business or working* arena and not inside their own homes and families. They tend to fall apart when the going gets rough at home, however, and at worst this can cost them the very thing that they most want. They do best when they ally themselves either to a calmer and more resilient partner or to a more adventurous one.

Cancerians, in common with the other two water signs, can be moody and difficult and they don't always know why they suddenly become angry, tense or sulky. They can be very manipulative as well, which makes them very difficult to live with at times.

Cancerians don't want to be difficult; they want to love and to be loved. They enjoy family life and they don't exclude their families from their working lives. They can be very demanding to live with because they need a bottomless pit of love and attention.

These people enjoy collecting things and they can be quite knowledgeable about history, historical objects or articles such as antiques, china, coins, Tarot cards and so on. They also love to save money and they hate debts. Cancerians are supposed to love the sea, but I think that they actually prefer the countryside. They definitely need to get out into open spaces from time to time. Many Cancerians love to travel and, although they need the security of a home base, they love getting away from it to explore new places. Cancerians can cling to their families and they can make it difficult for their children to leave home and become independent when the time comes.

——How the Sun Expresses Itself in Leo——

Leo is a masculine, fixed fire sign which is outgoing, generous and fun-loving in nature, but also stubborn and disinclined to give way on anything. Leo is ruled by the Sun itself, so the Sun is at its most comfortable in this sign. The Sun can express itself in its purest form, unadulterated by other considerations. For example, the Sun in Leo suggests that everything must have an element of fun or the feel of a game about it and even mundane family and business matters must have a touch of humour and glamour about them.

Sun in Leo People

Leos are proud; their standards are high and they are proud of all that they achieve. These people are not materialistic in the sense of needing lots of money in the bank or of having more than the Joneses, but they want everything life can offer and they usually set out to get it. They want to succeed and they want their families to be happy and successful too. An unsuccessful Leo or one who is going through a bad patch, can be very unhappy indeed but he has courage and a capacity for hard work, both of which help him to find a way of surviving bad times and coming out on top again as soon as he can. Leos are usually kind and generous, good natured and sociable but they can become mean and cranky if life doesn't go their way. These subjects can be restless, impatient and critical but they are often harder on themselves than they are on others. Leos have old-fashioned values, being basically honest, hard-working family people but there are some who are tricky to the point of being dishonest. A few are truly tyrannical.

These subjects need an adventurous life and a prestigious or glamorous line of work, but they will stick to a poor job if necessary, rather than be without work. Leos often choose jobs which allow them to travel or to get out and about and talk to people. Leos are not usually intellectual or academic. Their thinking is slow and rather inflexible and their ideas and interests quite mundane. However, if Mercury is in nearby Virgo, the mind is much quicker, with an academic, intellectual bent, with writing ability and a very quick wit. One of their greatest assets is their organisational talents and their sheer ability to get things done. Leos are not as dramatic or as outgoing as most astrologers seem to think, because they are easily embarrassed and they don't like to make a spectacle of themselves. Their kindness and sympathy can make them a soft touch for less scrupulous people.

——How the Sun Expresses Itself in Virgo——

Virgo is a feminine earth sign which is mutable in nature. It is concerned with detail, careful and diligent work, modesty and fussiness. The earthy element signifies that jobs are done thoroughly and carefully, while Mercury's rulership of Virgo means that they are done quickly and efficiently. A Virgoan attitude to the Solar concept of creativity would bring success in such things as needlework, light engineering, farming, writing or draughtsmanship.

Sun in Virgo People

Virgoans are hard to understand and sometimes difficult to live with because their personal standards are very high. Some

Virgoans are excessively tidy while others may work and live in a mess but they know exactly where everything is, and they get annoyed when anyone else tries to tidy up their stuff. These people are careful and discriminating, and they tend to be thorough in all that they do. Virgoans are extremely knowledgeable and they manage to combine having specialised knowledge in one or two subjects with a great deal of general knowledge as well. Some Virgoans have strangely split personalities, being sometimes extremely modest and retiring in some situations but very outgoing in others. Some Virgoans are defensive, unpleasant and very hard on others. These subjects can have what the Americans call an 'attitude problem' using their clever tongues as a social weapon. Others are kindly, gentle and witty, with a delightful sense of humour and a heart of gold. The nicest Virgoans are drawn to work in fields where they can help others. Their worst fault is self-destructiveness: they can get something going really well and then shoot themselves in the foot.

Virgos need a supportive partner to help them overcome their lack of confidence. They are extremely loving in a practical way, showing their love by doing things for their partners and children, rather than cuddling or playing with them. Oddly enough, this is a very sensual sign and these people can be very highly-sexed which is, of course, a practical way of showing love and affection. Virgos are dutiful parents and marriage partners but they can be very critical of others and they can spend too much time worrying or trying to cross bridges before they come to them. These subject are refined, humorous and very good to their friends. They are punctual, well organised, dependable and they are adaptable enough to fit in with any situation. Virgoans make wonderful friends because they have the time and patience to chat about anything and they are there for their friends whenever they need help.

——How the Sun Expresses Itself in Libra——

Libra is a masculine sign which is cardinal and airy in nature. It is concerned with balance, harmony and fair play, but it is also quite a tough and adventurous sign. The Sun in Libra expresses itself in a co-operative manner, and any enterprise would be carried out in as pleasant and charming a way as possible.

Sun in Libra People

Librans have a deceptive appearance and a slightly schizophrenic personality. Some look soft as butter while having a hard and determined core, while others appear tough but are great softies underneath. Most of them have a streak of resilience which sees them through. Librans can be very persuasive when selling things or when they want something for themselves. Many Librans, therefore, work as agents and they make excellent diplomats, lawyers and negotiators. Librans cannot take too much stress; they need a reliable career and a good relationship but they are more ambitious than they appear. Most of these subjects are spotlessly clean, they have excellent taste and appreciate the best of everything. Many of them work hard and climb the ladder of success in order to provide for themselves and their loved ones. Oddly enough, a large number of Librans choose to live in scruffy and dirty circumstances, never really getting their act together. There is a kind of astrological polarity operating here which suggests that issues relating to cleanliness and refinement need to be explored. The same goes for the polarities of organisation and disorganisation, laziness and diligence.

Some Librans have a problem with decision-making, while others simply need time to come to their conclusions. The reason for this shilly-shallying is that their finely-balanced legal minds tend to look at all sides of a question and to examine the fairness of their choices. They prefer to stop and think before committing themselves to anything. These subjects are very romantic and very flirtatious, and some of them have a real problem with fidelity. The unfaithful variety of Libran likes to keep his options open and to explore a variety of relationships while, at the same time, being safely and happily married. If the partner demands the same kind of freedom, these subjects become extremely jealous and would end a relationship immediately, rather than put up with the kind of compromise that they so cheerfully expect from others. Librans can be very miserable at times, but mostly they are cheerful, optimistic, humorous, good-natured and very sexy.

Librans are wonderful company and great talkers and, despite the fact that they aren't good listeners, they have the knack of understanding other people. One aspect of this sign which can be very irritating to others is their inability to see things as they are. These people seem to be able to believe whatever they want to, even when it is patently obvious that what they believe is simply not true. Some Librans become completely detached from reality.

—How the Sun Expresses Itself in Scorpio—

Scorpio is a feminine sign which is fixed and watery in character. Despite the feminine/water aspect it is a strong sign and everything about it is clear, definite and quite tough. There is a resilience and determination about this sign which permeates all that it touches. Anything that the Sun represents is done thoroughly and with great energy. Just one example of this would be the concept of fatherhood. Scorpio fathers take their role seriously and they don't abandon their children if they can possibly help it, but they may be a little heavy handed in their approach to discipline.

Sun in Scorpio People

Scorpios are reliable, resourceful, hard working and intensely loyal. They are extremely well-organised and they have 'filofax' minds. These subjects take life seriously and they make an effort in all that they do. The Scorpio motto is 'if you are going to do something, do it properly'. They expect others to be as thorough and as capable as themselves, and they may actually show contempt for those who aren't. Scorpios have a funny attitude to jobs and employers because they don't yearn for the status symbols of an executive position. They prefer to operate from a lower level as the power behind the scenes, controlling and manipulating without being seen to do so. Scorpios are excellent organisers.

They can make good but very difficult marriage partners because they don't always tell their partners what is on their minds. If these people have problems at work or in a social setting, they may release their tensions by behaving badly to their loved ones. These subjects can be secretive, possessive, controlling and dictatorial but there is a softer side to many of them, and they suffer badly when hurt. An unintentional snub may be considered a deep insult and a partner who countermands their directives can be seen as a traitor. Some Scorpios have a crusty exterior which puts people off, while others are very charming and likeable. Their deceptive appearance and manner often hides a kind and generous heart although, in truth, there are many Scorpios who relate better to animals than to people. If one takes the time to understand Scorpios, they make wonderful friends and the most loyal and dependable partners. Their feelings are very deep. They suffer from jealousy, deep-seated anger and bitterness and they have a totally unreasonable fear of abandonment. These inexplicable feelings may be carried forward from childhood experiences (or even previous life experiences). One either likes Scorpios or one doesn't! They want to be respected and they need standing up to because they loathe weakness in others. They fear their own human frailty and they don't often acknowledge their own fears, weakness or lack of self-esteem. They can also be far too honest, unable to say they like something when they don't, even when they risk offending someone by their honesty.

These subjects are often much more vulnerable than they appear and they are usually much better company than most astrology books would lead one to believe. Scorpios are extremely affectionate and also very playful. When they are happy, they can be the sunniest people around but, when they are sad, then everyone suffers. They can also be very clannish.

How the Sun Expresses Itself in Sagittarius

Sagittarius is a masculine fire sign which is mutable in character. Optimism, enthusiasm and the ability to look forward characterise this sign and the Sun expresses itself very energetically in Sagittarius. To give an example of the action of the Sun here, any new venture would be tackled enthusiastically and energetically, but they may try to do so much at once that nothing constructive emerges.

Sun in Sagittarius People

These people are pleasant, cheerful, optimistic and likeable. Their intense honesty can make them tactless and outspoken but they bear no grudges and any hurtful comments are made thoughtlessly and completely without malice. Some Sagittarians live very exciting lives, travelling, exploring and making new friends wherever they go while others seem content to plod along in a pedestrian job with a secure home life and nothing much coming along to rock the boat. Sagittarians themselves vary from energetic, fiery types to the kind of tall, rawboned, slow-moving people who seem to take life at a slow loping gate. Many Sagittarians love a sporty outdoor life and they are traditionally supposed to be especially interested in working with large animals. However, many of them have ordinary indoor jobs and confine their love of animals to the small domestic variety. These subjects enjoy working for large organisations where they can meet a variety of people, and they are very good at dealing with the public or with people who have problems. Some of these subjects are rather rebellious in childhood while others reject parental affection, others find it hard to fit in to their home or their school situation. Many Sagittarians have poor co-ordination and they can have silly accidents as a result.

There is a common belief that all Sagittarians love horses. This is just not true, as my friend Denise Stuart has discovered. She and I have between us some forty years' experience in astrology, and can only come up with one case of a Sagittarian who was horse-mad. The rest have been, on the whole, totally indifferent to them. Denise's theory is that before other forms of transport were available, Sagittarians were devoted to horses as a means of getting around. Now that we have fast cars and aeroplanes to give them the ability to move at a moment's notice, Sagittarians no longer need their poor old faithful steeds.

Both sexes are generous with their time and their possessions and they can be taken advantage of as a result of this. If a Sagittarian is let down or badly-treated, they can become surprisingly angry and unforgiving. Some Sagittarians need to work at grounding themselves or developing practicality. These people love to travel and to meet new people and they are never prejudiced on the grounds of race or religion, indeed they fight against such prejudice. Sagittarians can be great fighters for justice and fair play and their strong social conscience can lead them to work in the law or the Church.

How the Sun Expresses
Itself in Capricorn

Capricorn is a feminine sign which is cardinal and earthy in character. The Sun expresses itself in a steady and thorough manner in Capricorn, and so they do everything in a modest, charming but totally professional manner. To take a silly example; the Sun is concerned with gold and jewellery, therefore in Capricorn any gold products which are manufactured, bought or given would be of the finest and most tasteful quality.

Sun in Capricorn People

Capricorn folks are patient, realistic, responsible and hard working. They don't walk away from unpalatable situations lightly and they stick to marriages and partnerships as long as possible. However, this is a cardinal sign, not a fixed one, which means that they won't stay put for the sake of it, and they have the courage to face new situations as and when they arise. Capricorns are refined and gentle; they dislike rough or crude people and, most of all, they hate to be embarrassed. These subjects are ambitious, but they have the patience to wait for things to work out. They can be status-conscious but they avoid the flashier symbols of success. Wealthy Capricorns choose clothes which are quiet, refined and, wherever possible, expensive. Female Capricorns are extremely feminine in appearance and dress even when working in executive positions. They are interested in business and money and they often do well in later life. Such subjects may be shy when young but they gain confidence and become more sociable as they get older.

Capricorns make good marriage partners because they truly prefer to be settled in a happy family than flitting from one partner to another. These subjects are not as dull as they sound, however, because they have a wonderfully dry sense of humour and they can be quite flirtatious. They are often very good looking and, even if rather ordinary, they tend to look 'nice'. Capricorns can be insecure and they do best in life if they have an encouraging partner. Some Capricorns choose to live with the oddest of partners, sometimes choosing one who is much more outgoing and adventurous than themselves. These people are very good to their parents and parents-in-law, and they often have to put up with quite difficult older family members. Oddly enough, they can get into a state over quite small matters and they need a good friend to whom they can grumble from time to time. Friends of mine who have Capricorn partners tell me that they are very sexy!

How the Sun Expresses Itself in Aquarius

Aquarius is a masculine sign which is of the fixed air group. (Many people mistake Aquarius for a water sign because its symbol is a water carrier but it is, in fact, an air sign.) The Sun expresses itself in a cool, detached and independent manner in Aquarius and to give an example, any dealings with children would be carried out in a calm, reasonable and intellectual fashion.

Sun in Aquarius People

Aquarians are clever, friendly, kind and humane. They take a reasonable, unsentimental and impersonal attitude to most things, but they can get very worked up when things go wrong in their own lives. Friendship is often easier for these people than family life and some of them get on with animals better than people. Some Aquarians seem to live in a dream world, finding it hard to get anything done, or tackling too many things at one time to do any of them properly. Some Aquarians are very well-organised and extremely tidy while others are messy and unpunctual. These people are so individual that they are unlike anybody else, including other Aquarians! They march to their own drumbeat and live their lives in their own chosen manner. Some of them seem to live entirely inside their own heads, while others throw themselves into causes of one kind or another.

Aquarians make excellent teachers and they have a great deal of patience with anyone who is willing to learn. They can express themselves clearly and put points across to others in an imaginative manner. These apparently cool, calm people are actually quite tense inside and they can have stupendously bad tempers. Like Scorpios, they can walk over weaker people and they only really respect those who stand up to them. Aquarian minds are logical and their thinking is extremely broad, most of them are clever, some of them are very clever indeed. Some Aquarians need to develop sympathy and understanding and to come down from their ivory towers and get stuck into real life, but others are well able to cope with homes, jobs and families.

Many Aquarians work in the caring professions and their detached attitude makes them excellent counsellors or arbitrators. These subjects will help others for no reward and they make the most loyal and wonderful friends.

—How the Sun Expresses Itself in Pisces—

Pisces is a feminine water sign which is mutable in quality. The Sun can be a bit lost in this sign, because its watery, mutable nature is so different from the fiery, fixed Sun, but the Sun's energies can be bent towards such things as teaching, caring for others or delving into the metaphysical side of life. The creative energies of the Sun are used in a gentle manner and everything is done on a slow scale, unless there are tough modifying factors in the horoscope.

Sun in Pisces People

Pisceans are very hard to quantify because they can present themselves in so many guises. Most of them are quiet, gentle, kind and slow-moving, while some can be surprisingly fiery. Pisceans will rush to give practical help when it is needed but, despite their reputation for being caring, they don't make good listeners. Many of these subjects work in the psychic field because they're drawn to the hidden, mystical and occult features of this work although they are not particularly keen on the counselling or listening aspect of it. Their motivation is to develop self-awareness and to get in touch with 'spirit', rather than to spend their days listening to other people's aggravations. However, they love to go on at length about their own problems and to extract every ounce of attention possible from their family and friends!

These subjects have a reputation for being impractical but this is simply not so. They are often very good with their hands and, if one source of income dries up, they soon find another. Pisces people are creative and many of them are gifted artists or musicians. They can create a home out of nothing and they can make money like crazy when they have to. However, some don't bother to make money but simply find someone else to provide for them! Many Pisceans lack confidence and they are very vulnerable when young, but they gain strength and confidence in their decision-making abilities as they grow older. They do well if matched to a practical and supportive partner and they blossom in a happy family. However, many seem to miss the boat where emotional happiness is concerned. A surprising number of Pisceans go through long periods of promiscuity or, at other times, experience equally long spells of celibacy.

Pisceans tend to have larger than average families and they can be happy living in a rambling house filled with relatives, children and animals. Many of these subjects travel in order to escape from normality. Others bury themselves in a hobby or try to escape into drink or drugs. Some have a strong hold on life while others seem to have a very tenuous one. Few Pisceans fear the idea of dying and most believe in reincarnation or in salvation.

MOON SIGNS

The Moon's influence on a natal chart can be as great as that of the Sun or the ascendant. Some people, especially women, are more like their Moon sign than their Sun sign while they are young, but will often begin to move towards the character of their Sun sign after the Saturn return at the age of thirty.

————————Moon in Aries————————

These subjects are quick thinkers and talkers who are clever large-scale planners, but they need help with details. They are starters rather than runners, and they may be happier in an executive position than as one of the workers. Moon in Aries subjects can be tough go-getters but their confidence evaporates quickly and they need the support and admiration of others. Women with this placement need a career. Enthusiastic, headstrong and freedom-loving, they cannot take restriction or unnecessary discipline. Such people may have stormy love lives, either because they are changeable and easily bored, or because they are unwilling to compromise. However, they are usually honest and they don't try to manipulate others. Moon Aries subjects can be very deft and dexterous and their excellent co-ordination can make them successful at sports. The Moon is a water planet and when it is in a fire sign, emotions are expressed quickly and easily, but Moon-Ariens can have a very hot temper although they usually cool down again fairly quickly and don't sulk for long. Such people feel quite entitled to their emotions and are not shy about exhibiting them. In a way, I guess, what you see is what you get!

These subjects may have a hot-tempered parent, or parents who pushed them into competing and succeeding either at school or in sports. Some are brought up in a military atmosphere and many are drawn to the military life, or to working in large organisations with a definite structure. This placement does not suggest a bad or unhappy childhood but there can be considerable tension between the subject and the father. This seems to affect daughter/father relationships particularly badly. The Moon Aries subject can become quite a pushy and demanding parent in his own turn but he usually loves his children and genuinely wants the best for them.

Moon in Taurus

This is supposed to be a very stable and comfortable placement for the Moon, but I have noticed that these subjects are only stable and sensible when their lives are in perfect working order. They can deal with practical problems very efficiently, but when emotional problems come along, they fall apart quite easily and can even become suicidal. Moon Taurus subjects have a pleasant manner and they are sociable, respectable, reliable and decent. These subjects need a settled and happy family life, a comfortable home and a good job. They make good parents and successful family members. All the Moon-Taurus subjects that I have come across love music, and most love beautiful gardens, nature, the outdoors and travelling. They are loving, affectionate and romantic and some of them are strongly-sexed, whilst all of them are affectionate to those whom they love. They enter relationships with the best of intentions and only leave them if there is no other way to live. These subjects don't have many close friends and they are not always generous with time or money to people outside their own circle. Moon Taurus people can be possessive, jealous and stubborn, and they need stability and they seek to uphold the status quo. These people have formidable tempers and they can be very destructive if they feel threatened. They are tough but fair in business, and they can be quite fortunate financially.

Lunar Taureans may have a childhood which is materially comfortable but lacking in wholehearted love. They seem to have acquisitive mothers who instil a respect for material things. Their parents instill a need for educational qualifications and money, but they seem to be unwilling to offer emotional warmth, approval or security. If the mother was reasonable, the father may have had a weak character, poor health or, alternatively,.he may have been loud and tyrannical. Lunar Taureans can experience violence, either by being violent or by being on the receiving end of violent behaviour by others.

—————————Moon in Gemini—————————

These subjects have active minds which may be academic, creative, imaginative or logical, depending upon other features on the birthchart. They are dexterous and versatile and can cope easily with most tasks around the home. They work well under supervision as long as they respect their superiors. They need to feel free and some of them may avoid getting involved in permanent relationships altogether. However, those who do marry need a practical but easy-going partner. Some Moon Gemini subjects enjoy passive entertainment in the form of books, films and the television, while others enjoy more active pastimes such as sports. They have many friends. Many Moon in Gemini subjects work in typical Geminian jobs such as the travel trade, journalism or teaching. They are excellent teachers and they make good parents. Moon Gemini women need a job outside the home, although they are not bad homemakers. They remain youthful as they get older and they are usually up-to-date in their thinking.

This Moon placement can indicate a difficult childhood where the subject loses touch with one or more of his parents and is looked after by other people. If the home life was all right, there may have been difficulty in fitting in at school. These subjects may suffer from bullying both in and out of school. There is, however, a good side to a Lunar Gemini childhood and that is the intellectual stimulation which is on offer. These children may have at least one really unusual parent (usually the mother), and the childhood household is filled with books, newspapers, radios, televisions and interesting visitors. If these children are not abandoned, their parents will be the type to encourage education

and out-of-school activities. If you have children with the Moon
in air signs, make sure you have plenty of space in your house to
store their books, papers, videos, CDs, magazines, reference
directories, piles of notes, computers, cassette radios, video players
and all the rest of it.

──────────Moon in Cancer──────────

As the Moon is the ruler of the sign of Cancer, it is at its most
comfortable in this sign and its intrinsic characteristics are
heightened. These subjects are emotional, sensitive and moody.
They are usually imaginative and creative and they appreciate the
arts. Lunar Cancerians use intuition in daily life and they may be
drawn to study psychic and intuitive subjects. These people can
be emotionally demanding, requiring a bottomless pit of love and
attention, and they can make others feel guilty when caught failing
to meet these demands. Lunar Cancerians can be bossy,
manipulative and clever at piling on the emotional blackmail in
order to get their own way. Fortunately, not all of them are so
difficult and, even those who are may learn enough self-awareness
to modify their behaviour.

These subjects make good family members and excellent
parents and they are often drawn into teaching or other caring
professions. Both sexes are domesticated and many are excellent
do-it-yourselfers. They may be clannish, unwelcoming or
suspicious of strangers but, on the other hand, they may simply
be somewhat shy and nervous of the world outside their homes.
Lunar Cancerians are shrewd in business matters which, coupled
with their intuition and their capacity for hard work, can make
them very successful. They don't like taking chances and they need
financial and emotional security. They plan for their old age and
they often remain quite youthful in spirit even when old, but they
need the security of having a little money put by. They love the
sea and enjoy travelling with their families.

Moon in Cancer subjects normally have quite reasonable
parents and they are well-loved as children. They are usually closer
to their mothers than their fathers and they may be quite similar

in nature to their mothers. They rarely abandon their parents and they may cling to their own children in turn. They may even become 'parents' to their own parents by looking after them later in life.

Moon in Leo

These subjects have a kindly nature and a sunny disposition. They are friendly, approachable and welcoming. They are rarely hostile or suspicious. These people may be genuinely confident, but many merely display an appearance of confidence which covers shyness and uncertainty. Moon Leo subjects are loyal, loving and rather idealistic, only leaving a relationship if it becomes absolutely necessary. If they do leave, they make new relationships and attach themselves to another family fairly quickly. They are happiest in both personal and business relationships when they are understood, appreciated and admired. These subjects can put a partner on a pedestal expecting too much from them, and then be disappointed when the partner fails to pass the test of perfection. Moon Leos are good organisers who enjoy an orderly life. They can be bossy, arrogant and over-confident at times and helpless at other times, but they shoulder responsibility well and have good leadership qualities. Moon in Leo subjects may have the feeling that they are 'special' in some way. They may have been artistic or clever as children and their parents may have made much of this, leaving them with the feeling that they are superior to others in some special way.

The Lunar Leo childhood is usually good although there may be too much emphasis on religion, tradition or educational attainment. One parent, often the father, could be a tyrant and the Moon-Leo child may be so afraid of the parent that they never really get to know them. The mother is normally warm-hearted and energetic, and the childhood home is comfortable and well-organised. This is not normally a difficult Moon placement. Some of these subjects may be eager to please others but they don't have to work hard to win approval in the way that other, less fortunate, Moon sign subjects do.

----------------**Moon in Virgo**----------------

These subjects are keenly intellectual, discriminating and capable of dealing with details. They can work hard at a project that interests them, but they can also switch off and be surprisingly lazy. Probably the most important thing to bear in mind is that these people are *emotionally* contained. Sun or ascendant Virgo subjects are reserved, slow to push themselves forward. Moon Virgo subjects keep their emotions on a tight leash, so much so that they may never give themselves permission to express their real feelings. They may be embarrassed by displays of emotion or they may simply believe that they are not entitled to feel anything or to express anything freely. Strong emotions such as anger, jealousy, desire, love and hate may all be buried, denied or deflected into other activities, such as money-making, cleaning the home and so on. This may eventually erupt in fits of hysterics or it may turn inwards to make these subjects ill.

Moon Virgo folk are keen on matters related to health, hygiene, fitness and alternative therapies. They may be fussy or 'funny' eaters and they are often sensitive to certain types of foods, although many of these subjects are excellent cooks. Some Lunar Virgoans can be timid and full of worries, nerves and negativity, but most are actually quite confident and can be rather stubborn, awkward and determined. Some can be surprisingly opinionated and tactless. These subjects are conscientious providers and excellent at the practical sides of family life, but they may find it hard to show loving feelings to their partners or their children. Oddly enough, they are strongly sexual and they may be able to show love, affection and appreciation best by physically making love. This is great if the partner understands this, but not so wonderful if he/she doesn't. This tendency can also leave the kids out in the emotional wilderness. Don't forget, however, that these problems will be greatly modified by other factors on the birthchart.

These subjects make sacrifices for their families and they show their considerable feelings by *working* in order to provide their partners and their children with what they need. Lunar Virgo subjects are clever with money and they often make shrewd investments and purchases. They work in areas where they can use their communications skills while also helping humanity. Teaching, nursing and the media often attract them but some of them make wonderful businessmen and women.

Moon in Virgo subjects often have difficult childhoods, and this is probably behind a great deal of their self-contained, 'touch-me-not' attitude or their relationship problems. Some of them lack confidence and have a low sense of self-esteem, due to over-critical and over-demanding parents. The mother may be distant, too concerned with outer appearances and only willing to give love and approval when the child achieves something. Other Lunar Virgo subjects have parents (especially mothers) who simply cannot cope with life, and who may even degenerate into mental illness or terminal depression. Some Moon Virgo subjects become 'parents' to their own parents even while they themselves are still children. This is not an easy Moon placement! Fortunately, these subjects are not fools and if they take the trouble to look into the reasons behind their unhappiness, they can develop the kind of understanding which allows them to change and to grow.

Moon in Libra

These subjects are charming, optimistic, outgoing and sociable. They are skilled and tactful diplomats who are popular at work, and in all kinds of social settings. To cap all this, they are often very good-looking too. Lunar Librans can appear weak or soft, but they are often very hard workers and they have considerable determination when they have a particular goal in sight. These subjects don't enjoy being alone; they seek partnerships in business and personal life and they have many friends. In days gone by, these subjects got married when young, but nowadays they may live with a series of partners. They are faithful when in a relationship, but it is often quite hard for them to determine exactly what a relationship actually is! Moon Libra subjects need pleasant living and working surroundings and they are quite fussy about decor and colour schemes. They make excellent architects, interior designers and even software designers. Their diplomatic skills can take them into agency work, marketing or union negotiating. They make surprisingly tough business people. They may be quite artistic. Although happy-go-lucky and good company most of the time, they do have an unpleasant side. They can be arrogant, and they can argue the hind leg off a donkey; they don't back away from a fight and they make damned sure that they get their own way. For all their fussiness, they may be untidy. Some of these subjects disappear for hours on end, only reappearing at mealtimes. Some of them use their homes and families as a kind of 'pit-stop' on their way around the track of their interesting and self-indulgent lives.

A Moon-Libra childhood is usually a pleasant one, with kindly, clever parents who do all they can to stimulate the child's intellect. In some cases, the father is a distant figure. He may leave when the child is young or he may involve himself in business or other matters and leave the children in the hands of the mother. There is little strict discipline and everything is reasonable, including the child himself (most of the time)! These children may come under pressure to do well at school, because they are often rather lazy. The childhood home is probably full of books, music and intellectual stimulation.

Moon in Scorpio

Whenever the Moon is in a water sign, the emotions are intense and, in Scorpio, they are either well-hidden or close to the surface. These people are very 'into themselves' and they take their own feelings very seriously. If they are let down in love, they can drive their friends and family crazy by continually harping on about their disappointment. Other Lunar Scorpios may never mention their troubles but allow them to turn inwards so that they fester. They can make life difficult for themselves and, sometimes, for everyone else too. Lunar Scorpios can be moody, secretive and hard to understand. They don't forget those who hurt them, but they are intensely loyal and loving to those who are good to them, and they don't readily forget favours or obligations. These subjects hate to owe money and they hate those who borrow without paying them back. These people do best when allied to a cheerful, capable and emotionally-stable partner, but their own vulnerability can lead them to choose vulnerable, sensitive or, worse still, chaotic mates. Although stubborn and inclined to stick to their choices, they can be driven to leave a relationship, and they then learn from their mistakes and go on to make better choices in future. Sex can be used as a weapon. Magnetic, determined and manipulative, these people can be extremely fascinating in a dangerous way.

Lunar Scorpios struggle to achieve financial success and security but if they find themselves without either, they have the ability to pick themselves up and to start again. They love challenges and can put a lot into their careers, partnerships and children. They may experience great gains and losses, and can suffer extremes of tragedy or joy in their lives. They don't find it hard to attract friends, lovers or even money if they put their minds to it. Their intense emotions are usually kept away from their work colleagues, and they can be hard and steady workers in a variety of fields. Tough, masculine jobs appeal to some of them while the world of health and healing appeals to others.

The Moon in Scorpio can indicate childhood difficulties either in the home or at school. These children are intuitive and often artistic, and they may find the structure of mathematics or languages difficult to grasp although, once they get into art, music, medicine, building or engineering they pick themselves up very quickly. They learn to keep their thoughts to themselves, and they may have to cope with one or both parents being temperamental, unkind or unstable. They learn early on to hide their vulnerability and their true feelings.

Moon in Sagittarius

There are an astonishing number of people with the Moon in Sagittarius who work in the psychic field, and many are excellent astrologers, dowsers, palmists and just about anything else with a 'New Age' slant to it. It seems that the urge to explore takes an inward turn when the Moon is in this sign, leading these people to seek enlightenment at a deep and inner level. Superficially, Lunar Sagittarians are optimistic, outgoing and very friendly. Many of them travel a great deal or have strong connections to people from lands, cultures or backgrounds which are very different from their own. They seek to learn from these people or by visiting their lands. Most Lunar Sagittarians feel the need to contact as many people as they can during their lifetime and this may lead them to choose jobs in teaching or dealing with the public. Astrology, of course, is one way of doing this! These subjects need personal freedom and they may find marriage and commitment too confining but they can keep a friendship going for years. Many of these people are better at friendship than family life, while others relate well to animals. They may find it hard to stick at anything, but they can be happy if they can find a job or a lifestyle which offers them plenty of variety. Lunar Sagittarians may have pleasant but distant relationships with their parents, children, ex-partners and just about everyone else. These subjects are surprisingly ambitious and they can be quite competitive, which may lead some of them into a sporting lifestyle. They gamble on life, love, people, work, the horses and anything else which takes their fancy and, when something doesn't work out, they simply move on.

These subjects may have strange childhood experiences in which they are made to feel apart or distanced from those who are around them. They rarely receive enough nurturing, and they miss out on cuddles and affection. They try to catch up on this later in life by having a number of close relationships and some very good friendships which have a strong element of affectionate caring. They may not stick to one partner for life but they have the ability to draw others to them so they are rarely alone for long. Lunar Sagittarians can do well at school, but they often do most of their studying *after* leaving school.

──────────Moon in Capricorn──────────

The chances are that the Moon in Capricorn subject learned that life was hard from an early age. As children, these subjects are usually loved and wanted, but they may come from family circumstances which were difficult in some way. If the subject himself does not experience severe difficulties in childhood, it is likely that his mother would have. Either way, the messages which are passed on to these people are that hard work is important and that they must strive to find emotional and financial satisfaction from within themselves rather than by leaning on others. The emotions may actually be stunted due to childhood circumstances. They may be extremely shy, suspicious and clannish and it can take a long time before these subjects gain courage and confidence in themselves to open up to others. They may find an outlet in a career or a happy family life later on and they can overcome most of their problems by patient stoicism.

Lunar Capricorns are ambitious and they may not always be too careful about how they achieve their ambitions. Power or money can be seen as a compensation for emotional emptiness. These subjects have a responsible attitude to life and they rarely abandon their families or friends. They have a good sense of humour and they are able to laugh at themselves, but they can be touchy and they don't care to have others laugh at them. They are usually long-lived and they make up in old age for the unhappiness or insecurity of their childhood. Some Lunar Capricorns are emotional loners. They may have many colleagues and acquaintances but few real friends and no real partnerships.

Moon in Aquarius

Lunar Aquarians need independence in their marriages and their careers. They cannot live under someone else's thumb or be dictated to by others. If any of these subjects have to face a particularly difficult situation, they prefer to do this on their own, without an audience. For example, when a Lunar Aquarian friend of mine went into hospital for bypass surgery, he wouldn't even allow his wife to come and visit him until it was all over and he was feeling and looking 'presentable'. Lunar Aquarians of both sexes need an interesting career and many of them are happy to work for themselves. These subjects are very imaginative and they can be extremely creative. They certainly have plenty of ideas to pass on to others and there is nothing they like better than to be asked for their advice. Under stress, these subjects can become gossipy, aloof or sarcastic and they are, at all times, unpredictable.

These people are broadminded, always up-to-date and they are keen to live their lives to the full. They can be quite tough to live with because of their extreme independence and their self-contained attitude. They can be obstinate, awkward, argumentative, determined and keen to have their own way. They need a partner whom they can respect, for if they don't they will walk all over them. However, they do need to relate to people both as friends and in a close and loving way, and they will do their utmost to help their partners. These people are loyal and steadfast and often very kind; they want to help others and they tend to attract lame ducks. Many have a strangely distant relationship with their parents, while others are forced to take on the job of parenting their own parents while they, themselves, are still very young.

Moon in Pisces

This is a strange placement which can lead the subject into a really unusual lifestyle. Many Lunar Pisceans are mystical, psychic and extremely sensitive. When I served on the committee of the British Astrological and Psychic Society, all nine of us had the Moon in Water signs. Two had the Moon in Cancer and the rest of us were Lunar Pisceans! I once worked at a psychics and mystics fair where everybody around me had either the Sun, Moon or ascendant in Pisces, and two of the consultants had both the Sun and Moon in Pisces! This Moon placement leads to a great deal of vulnerability and shyness, but this is often covered up well, especially in later life. There is often something very wrong in childhood and the Lunar Piscean may feel extremely lonely throughout childhood and for a long time afterwards, even when they are actually surrounded by people. Lunar Pisceans may actually choose to be alone for much of the time, because the continual presence of other people can upset the delicate balance of their aura. These subjects act as psychic sponges, picking up the moods and vibrations of all with whom they come into contact.

In some cases, low self-esteem leads to apathy and an inability to get anything done, but when these indecisive worriers have the support of a strong, steadfast and reliable partner they can blossom. If loved and cared about, the Lunar Piscean offers love, devotion and faithfulness on a level which few others can provide. Sympathetic, romantic and loving, these generous people may be too soft and delicate to cope with the rough-and-tumble of daily life. However, many of these subjects have a tensile inner strength which comes to the fore in times of crisis, and they have a truly magical gift for helping those who are troubled. Timid, retiring and possibly suffering from poor health, these strange people often achieve more, show more courage and cope with far more than all the other Moon signs of the zodiac put together.

MERCURY

The best way to look at Mercury is to learn what the planet is all about and to understand how it works when in each of the signs. The section below offers an overview of this planet through the signs, but time and experience will show you many more variations.

————Mercury in Aries————

The mind is impulsive, quick-witted and the tongue can be sharp and sarcastic. There is often a good memory, particularly for poetry, literary quotations or quiz trivia. The nature is self-assertive and there is a fighting spirit. These subjects can be nervous, impulsive and hyperactive. They may act first and then think later. They can concentrate on something which interests them, but they tend to skip lightly over other things without studying them deeply. Some Mercury in Aries subjects are highly intellectual.

Mercury in Taurus

The mind is retentive and the thought processes slow but logical. Learning may be easier through pictures than words. This subject is dexterous and practical and may be better with his hands than with academic subjects. Sensible and cheerful, but possibly a bit slow and stodgy, this person can be very stubborn and inflexible and incapable of lateral thinking. If nearby planets are in Gemini, this placement acts as a settling or grounding factor.

Mercury in Gemini

Mercury rules the sign of Gemini, so its character is almost pure in this sign (as it would also be in Virgo). These subjects are clever, versatile, inventive, quick thinking and gossipy. They can think on their feet and make lightning decisions, but they find it hard to concentrate on one thing at a time without a host of others crowding in. They are excellent communicators who are quick to learn, and they are happy using modern communications machinery. They can be easily bored and, thus, may prefer jobs either with plenty of variety, or where they move from place to place. Highly-strung and nervous, they may talk too much when under stress. Denise Stuart tells me that an afflicted Mercury in Gemini or in the third house, or a retrograde Mercury close to the ascendant, can be linked to severe dyslexia. A badly-placed Mercury can also be associated with stammering, brain damage, mental handicap, asthma and anything else which decreases communications ability.

Mercury in Cancer

These subjects may live in the past and they may take an interest in history or in objects which have historical associations. Their memory is excellent, but they are opinionated, intuitive and tenacious and they can harbour grudges. Kind, thoughtful and loyal, they dislike major change but they do enjoy novelty and a change of scene from time to time. These subjects can be very in

tune with their own bodies and they may be slightly inclined to
hypochondria.

──────────── Mercury in Leo ────────────

Cheerful, optimistic and creative, these subjects can be conceited,
arrogant and unfeeling towards others at times. Good public
speakers or teachers, they can be strong minded and tough in
business. They are excellent organisers but they are inclined to get
involved in over-optimistic schemes, or carried away with
glamorous but unrealistic projects. On the whole, however, these
subjects are fairly sensible and they are also generous and kind
hearted.

──────────── Mercury in Virgo ────────────

Mercury is the ruler of Virgo (as well as Gemini), therefore, it is
expressed in its purest form here. However, in Virgo it is associated
with the more academic, analytical and medical matters, in
addition to the all the ideas attached to communicating. Such
subjects are analytical, shrewd and practical, being good at
specialisation and problem-solving. The subject is an excellent
learner with a precise mind, but he may not be creative unless
there are planets in nearby Leo. This person may be an excellent
writer or journalist but he may also be a long-winded talker.
Extremely critical, although far more self-critical than critical of
others, but also well-informed, educated, (often self-educated),
and academic. He may have an affinity to the suffering of others,
due to having suffered himself, and is interested in healthy living,
possibly to the point of hypochondria.

──────────── Mercury in Libra ────────────

Romantic, gentle and tactful, these subjects make excellent
ambassadors. They have excellent taste in decor with a strong
sense of colour and are possibly good do-it-yourselfers. These
people love their creature comforts and may be inclined to be lazy.

They have good business sense, but they may lose opportunities through idleness. Sociable and humorous, they can be great fun.

────────────Mercury in Scorpio────────────

The mind is sharp and critical and there may be tendencies towards manipulation, suspicion, jealousy or possessiveness. These subjects may be interested in medical matters, the police or military subjects, and they can be excellent historians or specialists in any of the above. Some subjects can be cruel or immoral, whereas others are real softies who work hard for humanity. All love to say things which shock others! They can be clever in business but their tendency towards boredom and restlessness may make them lose interest, or forget to tie up loose ends. Some are filled with fears and phobias, while others seem to be carrying around a great deal of anger associated with long past events. They tend to be secretive, controlling and emotional rather than logical.

────────────Mercury in Sagittarius────────────

Some of these subjects do well at school, college, or university, while others 'misfire' when young, but educate themselves later. Broad-minded and lacking in prejudice, these people are interested in everything and everyone. They may find it hard to concentrate and they may be involved in so many things that they never really grasp or finish any one of them. Frank, versatile and restless, friendly and non-hostile, they love travel, foreigners and anything unusual. Some of these subjects are sportsmen and women, while others are drawn to religious or philosophical lifestyles due to their attraction to mystical or spiritual matters.

────────────Mercury in Capricorn────────────

Rational, practical, careful and patient; these subjects take life seriously. They must guard against melancholy and allow their dry, witty sense of humour to be their saving grace. Their minds are scientific and mathematical, or attuned to business. Some are keen linguists while others make excellent teachers. These subjects are traditional in outlook, reliable in business and kind hearted and loyal friends. They do their duty!

——————————Mercury in Aquarius——————————

Intuitive, inventive, modern, and interested in modern sciences and social progress, these subjects are excellent communicators who may choose to work with or for the public. A detached attitude makes them appear to be good judges of human behaviour but they may be too distanced to really understand others. They can also have eccentric ideas and an unrealistic outlook. These subjects can be very cutting and even quite cruel.

——————————Mercury in Pisces——————————

Intuitive, imaginative, flexible and kind, the minds of such subjects are broad and their thinking is drawn to mysticism, spirituality and the meaning of life and the afterlife, with possible tendency to be clairvoyant or spiritual. They can be chaotic and prone to escapism through drink, drugs, sex or constant travel. Over-emotional, secretive and extremely manipulative, these subjects lack confidence and they will give way in an argument, but they then find ways of getting back at their attacker or of going their own way regardless. There may be a flair for medicine or an interest in health or spiritual healing. These people are drawn to the entertainment business and they can be talented or artistic, while some are quite sporty. These subjects have a reputation for kindness but they can also be quite unpleasant.

VENUS

As with Mercury, this section offers you an overview of Venus through the signs but your own experience will add plenty more as time goes by. This planet can describe the kind of woman that a man is looking for. For example: Venus in Scorpio = passion, commitment, deep spirituality.

————Venus in Aries————

Strongly sexual, affectionate and fond of giving unusual presents, these subjects enjoy social life and outings. They are creative, popular and flirtatious, and can be headstrong and reckless with money, fluctuating between generosity and meanness. They may gamble or drink. Although not necessarily bothered about possessions, they may collect interesting items.

————Venus in Taurus————

Venus is the ruler of Taurus so its action is pretty pure when in this placement. Subjects are loving and passionate with a strong sensual streak which may be expressed by such things as cooking and eating, or a love of music and art or craftwork. Some are very keen on sex. These people make good hosts or hostesses. They can be self-indulgent but shrewd with money and in business matters, possessive about things and people, careful with money and probably mean. They tend to obtain and then hang on to property and goods, and they need a nice home and garden.

————Venus in Gemini————

Flirtatious, lighthearted, restless and possibly fickle, some of these subjects feel trapped by close personal relationships. They may be attracted to relatives such as cousins, etc. (I know of one who married his own niece!) They love travel, music, art and drama. Although adaptable to circumstances, they are often the odd one out in the family. They collect books or communications equipment although they are actually more interested in ideas than in things.

Venus in Cancer

Affectionate and sympathetic, they may tend to smother loved ones or lean on them. Emotional, clinging, imaginative, these subjects react badly to loss or rejection. They are homeloving, good cooks and good hosts although this will be less so if there are neighbouring planets in Gemini. They like history and antiques and need a nice home and garden. They can spend their lives searching for security of various kinds. They are happiest with a home-loving partner and plenty of money in the bank. These subjects must guard against weight gain.

Venus in Leo

These subjects need to feel deeply in love, but, although they adore their partners, they may also try to dominate them. These subjects are extravagant, generous, dramatic, and natural showmen. They love children, and also the arts and wearing rich clothes. These subjects need to express themselves in a creative manner, are inclined to be flirtatious and they need to be admired or appreciated. These subjects need some money behind them and they usually obtain property and goods along the way.

Venus in Virgo

They can be critical of their partners which can lead to problems in relationships but they can be even more critical of themselves, and this leads to low self-esteem. These subjects can find sex distasteful or grubby in some way, but alternatively, they can be very highly-sexed indeed. They are at their best in a safe, close and loving relationship where the partner is totally trusted. They could have an aversion to being touched by strangers, and although they are reserved and quietly charming, they may also be fault finding or fussy. They have good practical business abilities and they can be shrewd negotiators. Money is liked but these people are generous and they are not hoarders.

———————————**Venus in Libra**———————————

Gentle, lovable, sympathetic and sociable, these subjects are soft, kind and self-indulgent. Both sexes are good looking with really lovely eyes. They may fall in and out of love easily and they may find it hard to maintain one strong relationship, especially if this requires effort. Fond of creature comforts, sensitive and affectionate, these subjects are great company for a partner who is prepared to support them. Despite all this gentle laziness, these subjects have good business instincts and they co-operate well with stronger colleagues and partners. Artistic and musical, their taste is wonderful and their sense of line and colour can make them successful in the fashion or cosmetic industry. These subjects may not value possessions greatly but they cannot live in a mess or in an unpleasant environment.

———————————**Venus in Scorpio**———————————

Men with this placement are the kind who are written about in bodice-ripping novels: 'His blue-black curls fell over his brow, shielding deeply-set, intense blue eyes and, as he watched her reactions, his full lips curled into a smile which held just a hint of cruelty'. Women would be femmes fatales of the Mickey Spillane kind: 'She came at me in pieces. Firm thighs and hard concave stomach undulating at me from across the room'. Lovely stuff, eh?

Sensual, passionate and possessive, these subjects hang on to what is theirs, and they don't forgive a hurt. The up-side of this placement is that these subjects have very strong feelings and that their love is deep and genuine. They can also be extremely generous. They often have executive ability but their pig-headed attitude can spoil their efforts. Some of them are jealous of the ability of others. They are not especially acquisitive, being more interested in a good lifestyle than in accumulating things. These subjects make good and loyal friends and they can sometimes be taken advantage of by unscrupulous persons. This placement also indicates strong intuition, with possible clairvoyant powers and a need to be close to the spiritual side of life.

Venus in Sagittarius

These subjects need to feel free and they often choose a job or a way of life which allows them to take off whenever they feel like it. They may remain single and fancy-free longer than most. They are mildly flirtatious and very friendly. Some are adventurous in love while others are spiritual and somewhat virginal. These subjects are generous, idealistic and humanitarian. They can be inconsiderate, tactless and hypersensitive. They are drawn to travel and adventure and they link themselves to partners who lead interesting lives. There is no real interest in possessions but money may be needed for travel or hobbies. The subject could be attracted to partners from the world of sport, teaching or spirituality.

Venus in Capricorn

Conventional and stable in matters of affection, these subjects make excellent, if rather formal, marriage partners. They can be undemonstrative and rather serious but this is an earth sign, so their sexuality is likely to be quite strong. These subjects may be calculating and fussy at work and they can also be status-conscious. On the whole, they are thorough and reliable workers who will get on with things in peace. It is only when they are challenged that they dig in their heels and surprise others by fighting back hard. They usually have good sense and a shrewd commercial mind. These subjects are homeloving and somewhat acquisitive but they value such matters as education and the opportunity to appreciate the arts, travel or literature.

Venus in Aquarius

These subjects may balk against the restrictions of marriage or of a conventional job. They like to feel that they can come and go as they please. Generally speaking, they can cope with anything and they often have to do so. Detached, friendly and independent, they make excellent friends but rather cool lovers. They can be manipulative, and they may have their eye on the main chance. Helpful to friends and family, they hate to be smothered and they won't smother others. In common with anybody who has anything in Aquarius, these subjects may have some peculiar ideas. Possessions are not as important as being with someone who shares the subject's ideas and understands his/her needs. These subjects may lack passion.

——————Venus in Pisces——————

These subjects may be very creative, artistic or musical and they are most probably very good-looking. They are emotional, sentimental and very loving. They either need a creative outlet or one which allows them to express themselves. They may sacrifice all to a loved one or to their families. Some of these subjects are hopeless with money while others are very sensible indeed. Similarly, some are generous while others are tight-fisted. These people may appear to have a face value which is different from what is in their hearts, and they can be misunderstood.

MARS

As with all the planets, this is an overview which you will add to as you live and learn. The position of Mars in a woman's chart can show the kind of man she is attracted to.

——————Mars in Aries——————

Aries is ruled by Mars, so its energies are expressed in a pure manner in this sign. Aggressive, argumentative, outspoken, impulsive and obstinate, such subjects can be a real handful. They may appear self-assured on the surface, but they may actually be quite unsure of themselves underneath. There is a small child hidden not too far under the surface and it is this which makes them so attractive. Other attractive features are their openness and friendliness, in addition to their intelligence and their witty sense of humour. These subjects frequently have practical and mechanical abilities, they love gadgets and they may be attracted to the world of computers. Some are keen on a life in the armed services. They are very loving and they can be great fun, if one can stand the pace. They may be prone to fevers, eye troubles and accidents to the head.

Mars in Taurus

These people are hard practical workers who have the strength of character and obstinacy to finish what they start. Some of these subjects are good singers or dancers, and many are clever cooks, gardeners or craft workers. These people have a smouldering and somewhat grudging temperament, and they don't like to be opposed or deflected from their chosen path. Passionate about life and love, they have strong feelings which are not always apparent to others and they can be secretive and quite difficult to live with. These subjects have excellent organising talents and shrewd business abilities. They like money and they love sex. The throat is sensitive and the neck is prone to 'whiplash' accidents or spondilitis.

Mars in Gemini

Clever, talented and dexterous, these subjects may not have the staying power to finish what they start. Talkative, restless and nervous, they need a life which does not give them too many problems. These subjects are clever inventors and problem-solvers but they are easily bored by too much routine or detail. They are adaptable and interested in travel and communications. There may be a tendency to accidents to the hands, shoulders and arms.

Mars in Cancer

Tenacious, ambitious and clinging, emotional, sensitive and sensuous, these subjects need security and they need to be loved and cared for. Both sexes are domesticated and may be good at cooking, do-it-yourself jobs and creative gardening. These people make excellent but rather possessive parents and marriage partners and they may also be inclined to lean on their spouses. Very intuitive and probably psychic, these subjects are frequently attracted to the occult. They may have weak stomachs or (if female), sensitive breasts.

Mars in Leo

Enthusiastic, apparently fearless and keen on leadership, these subjects are go-getters. They like excitement and change and cannot put up with a dull or routine job. They enjoy travel, meeting new people and tackling a variety of problems. They appear confident but this may be something of a pose. Some of these subjects are overbearing or disciplinarian in outlook. They are attractive and popular and they have quite magnetic personalities. There may be problems with the spine or the heart.

Mars in Virgo

These subjects should be hard workers but sometimes they spend more time talking and fiddling about than actually doing anything. However, when their interest is aroused, they can get on extremely well and at great speed. These people need a job which holds their attention and which provides them with plenty of variety because boredom is their worst enemy. They are quite shrewd operators and they are capable of attending to details. They are drawn to work in the communications or medical industries. These people can be too critical and too nervous, with a tendency to worry about nothing. They can be difficult to live with because they may be fussy and demanding. Some have a dreadful mindless form of 'verbal diarrhoea'. Worry can make these subjects ill and, if this happens, they can develop skin or bowel problems.

─────────────Mars in Libra─────────────

These subjects are clever and perceptive about people. They are interested in communicating with others and they may be good business men and women. These people are friendly and sociable but they can be very laid back and rather lazy. They have a strong survival instinct and they will fight hard for what is theirs. Mars in Libra people are flirtatious and very fond of the opposite sex. Their marriage-type relationships should have a strongly sexual content. Their weak spots are the kidneys, pancreas and bladder.

─────────────Mars in Scorpio─────────────

Mars is the old ruler of Scorpio which means that its energies are not altered much by being in this sign. These subjects have very strong characters and they can bully weaker types. They aim high and work hard for their chosen goals. They can be secretive, relentless and even cruel at times. These people are very perceptive, intuitive and even quite psychic. They may be interested in the occult or anything else which is hidden. Some choose to work as detectives while others are drawn to the military life. They need to learn self-discipline and to have an organised lifestyle. As far as health is concerned, they are very strong and resilient, but they can drink too much and they may suffer spinal or reproductive problems.

─────────────Mars in Sagittarius─────────────

Boisterous and energetic, these people may take life by storm. They are independent thinkers who may choose unusual or unconventional lifestyles. Some are sceptical and questioning, while others are drawn to mysticism and astrology. These subjects love travel, sports and adventure. Some are outspoken, tactless and argumentative, while others use their intellect to fight injustice wherever they see it. Some Mars in Sagittarius people never really settle down but drift from one partner to another throughout their lives. Some are very sexually experimental. Their weak spots are the hips, thighs and arteries.

─────────Mars in Capricorn─────────

Subjects with Mars in Capricorn are strong characters. They may be ambitious, power hungry and obstinate, and they won't allow anything to get in the way of their ambitions. These subjects are practical, self-reliant and capable, with executive and organising ability. They can be cold, distant, irritable and unpleasant, but they do get things done. These people cannot tolerate waste and they do their duty as and when it is required of them. If they get a bee in their bonnets, nothing will deflect them from their chosen course. They are physically strong but they may suffer from problems with ears, teeth, bones, knees and skin.

─────────Mars in Aquarius─────────

These subjects are impulsive, intellectual and idealistic. They may be impatient and also very obstinate and determined. They may be keen on working for good causes. These people can be excellent in an emergency but otherwise, they are unpredictable. They can be emotionally frustrated or unable to express their emotions. They need freedom and they have a strong urge to reform the world around them. If they have any health problems, these would affect their ankles and the circulation through their legs.

─────────Mars in Pisces─────────

Some of these subjects are self-sacrificing, emotional and lacking in drive or concentration. Others are artistic and creative. They could be exceptional designers or engineers. They do have a dreamy side to them and this can be expressed in a love of ballet, culture or the arts. These people can be confused and chaotic, penny-wise and pound-foolish. They are successful when they are able to work on their own projects and develop their own ideas. Some are psychic, spiritual or mediumistic. The weak spots are the lungs, the feet and the circulation.

JUPITER

Jupiter takes a year to pass through one sign so it influences all those who are born within that year. This ties up quite nicely with Chinese astrology which takes into account the year, month and hour of birth.

————————Jupiter in Aries————————

Self-sufficient, freedom-loving, honest and extravagant, these subjects can be overly optimistic, reckless or thoughtless, and this can sometimes spill over into bullying other people. They need to learn to budget their time, money and energy. They can be good entrepreneurs, they can also do well in large, well-structured organisations. They value their self-sufficiency and the freedom to express their personal opinions, but they also value the organisations to which they belong.

————————Jupiter in Taurus————————

These people love comfort, rich living and good food, and they may overindulge in all of these things. They have sound judgement and their feet are on the ground. They are, for the most part, good-hearted, reliable friends and steady workers. They can be possessive or materialistic. They enjoy practical work, especially if it is on a large scale, such as construction work or landscape gardening. These people value what they can see, hear, feel, taste and touch.

————————Jupiter in Gemini————————

These subjects are clever but they may be superficial. They make good teachers and journalists. They are affable but unreliable as friends. Mentally alert, versatile and good conversationalists, they need constant stimulation because they are easily bored. They enjoy word games and literature and they are also dexterous and inventive. They can be crafty! They value thoughts and ideas as well as intellectual freedom, and they love to travel and to explore.

Jupiter in Cancer

These subjects are kind and good-humoured, protective and sympathetic. They are more ambitious than one realises and they can be quite restless. These people are emotional by nature and they can become emotionally attached to a business, a house, an area or an idea. They are sociable, patriotic and fairly old-fashioned in their values. Such people are loyal to their families but their possessiveness and touchiness can make them hard to live with. They may draw invisible lines which one crosses at one's peril. These subjects have good business sense but they can incline towards nepotism. They can make money from antiques and they value both things and people, especially members of their own family.

Jupiter in Leo

These subjects are big-hearted, generous and creative. They are often popular and they have the ability to draw people to them and to be loved by many. These people are intelligent, honest and vital and they like to live in a glamorous or exciting world. They can be overbearing, pompous and arrogant or big-headed. They enjoy prestige and money and they like to do everything on a grand scale. They need to be admired and they will try to produce work or to have a lifestyle which draws the attention of others. They may choose to work with young people or to teach or train others. These humorous people enjoy music and dancing and they feel that life is for living.

Jupiter in Virgo

These people are kind, conscientious, moral and ethical. They have an analytical approach to their work. They should try not to bottle up their emotions or divert too many of their feelings into their work. They enjoy research, analysis and intellectual pursuits. They may have success in the medical or scientific fields. They can be critical, pernickety or absent-minded. These people value material goods, money, education and ideas.

Jupiter in Libra

These subjects are sympathetic, kind, harmonious and charitable. They work best in a partnership or as part of a team, although they can be lazy and self-indulgent. They are interested in legal matters and may work in that field. They enjoy music, art, literature and culture. They need to be admired or praised and they value marriage and companionship.

Jupiter in Scorpio

These people can be very highly sexed and they may live life to the very fullest. They can be dramatic and self-centred. These subjects are shrewd, ambitious and strong-willed. They can overwork or, indeed, overdo almost anything to which they set their minds. These people can be proud and conceited but they can also relate to the underdog or to the animal world. They love a challenge and they enjoy seeking out things that are hidden, solving mysteries and solving problems. Some subjects are very drawn to the occult. They can make good policemen or thriller writers. They value personal achievement and strength of character.

Jupiter in Sagittarius

Sagittarius is under the rulership of Jupiter, so it expresses itself in a particularly pure manner in this sign. These subjects are optimistic, forward-thinking and philanthropic. They may choose to work in Jupiterian careers such as the law, the church or the travel trade. They are supposed to like large animals, but they seem to actually prefer small ones. These people are sympathetic and kind, but they may be erratic and tactless. They are broad-minded and they enjoy travelling or being in the company of foreigners. Most of them enjoy visiting wide open spaces. They may be a bit lazy and inclined to let things drift or they may jump from one idea to the next without getting anything done. Many of these subjects are intuitive and interested in astrology or the psychic and mystical world. They value personal freedom, independence and intelligence.

——————Jupiter in Capricorn——————

These subjects are resourceful, responsible and thoughtful. They can be stingy, penny-wise and pound-foolish, austere and cold. On the other hand, they can be thoughtful, productive and thorough. They work hard and may put their jobs before personal relationships. Some of these subjects can be egotistical, unsociable and unpopular, but they are deep thinkers and they value structure and old-fashioned ideas. They may value the Earth and all that is in it, and they may seek to save it in practical ways.

——————Jupiter in Aquarius——————

Humanitarian, impartial and imaginative, these subjects can be tactless, unpredictable, restless or obstinate and wilful. They are high-minded, idealistic and attached to causes but they may be unrealistic. These subjects need a definite goal to focus upon. They can be extremely intuitive and very attracted to astrology or the occult. They work hard on group projects. They value freedom, intellect and working for the betterment of the world.

——————Jupiter in Pisces——————

This is a good placement for work in the medical or the caring professions. These subjects are intuitive, imaginative and artistic. They are kind, humane, romantic and idealistic but they can become detached from reality. These people need a definite goal. They can be psychic, spiritual and attracted to the occult.

SATURN

Saturn stays in a sign for about two years which gives it something of an influence over a particular era, in addition to its influence on individual charts.

Saturn in Aries

This results in a see-saw personality which can be nice or nasty depending upon mood. These subjects are ambitious, determined and self-reliant. They can be defiant, jealous or impatient. They have good mechanical ability and they may be interested in military matters. They may have had a sarcastic, violent or destructive parent or possibly a tough time at school. They may have difficulty in expressing themselves or in being themselves. They can, however, achieve enormously high esteem. (Some of the more unpleasant aspects of Saturn in Aries may have been experienced *by* the subject as a result of childhood difficulties or a hard marriage, rather than being an expression of his own character).

Saturn in Taurus

Patient, cautious, methodical, economical and frugal, these subjects can be obstinate but they also have great perseverance and may work hard to produce things of beauty. They work well under pressure. These subjects may have had over-materialistic parents. There may be a background or a family history of poverty or of living in uncongenial places.

Saturn in Gemini

Logical, conscientious, shy and serious, these subjects can be deeply intellectual and also very dexterous. They have the patience to complete long and complicated tasks (like writing books!). These subjects are good at mathematics, science and, possibly, astrology and they make thorough and well-prepared teachers. Their early education may be unsuccessful but they never stop learning and they tend to catch up on what they missed at school. The father (sometimes mother) may have died or left the family in childhood. There could have been considerable loneliness in childhood which drove the child on an inward journey or took it into the world of books and imagination. Some of these subjects are very frightened in childhood due to bullying at home or at school — or both.

──────Saturn in Cancer──────

Shrewd, ambitious, tenacious and hard working, these subjects are very attached to their families and they may try to control them. These people are emotionally controlled and they can become melancholy or self-absorbed. One of the parents or parent figures could have made the childhood home unhappy.

──────Saturn in Leo──────

This subject could be self-assured or very self-effacing depending upon how Saturn affects them. There is excellent organising ability and a natural attitude of authority. Some find it hard to relax and enjoy themselves. Some have bad-tempered parents or ungrateful children.

──────Saturn in Virgo──────

These subjects are methodical, prudent and tidy but they can be critical, fault-finding and mistrustful. They have high personal standards and they are good at keeping confidences. They tend to mistrust the motives of others. They may have had cold or over-demanding parents.

──────Saturn in Libra──────

These subjects can be lonely, due to failed partnerships, even though they are kind, pleasant and honourable. They can work hard for a chosen goal or in order to right an injustice. Their parents would have been reasonable but there is a possibility that one parent abandoned his or her duties or deserted the family.

Saturn in Scorpio

This can be a very good or a really nasty placement! These people are resilient and capable; they have executive ability and a shrewd idea of what will and won't work. They can brood or hold a grudge and they may try to punish others. They can be either ruthless and inflexible or soft-hearted and impractical. They are capable of extreme jealousy, and they need opportunities for emotional or sexual release. In some cases, the problems don't belong with the subjects themselves but to their parents.

Saturn in Sagittarius

This is quite a good placement for Saturn because it steadies the daftness of Sagittarius, and loses some of its own intrinsic dourness in the process. However, it can signify a hurtful and tactless nature or a dedication to strange causes. (This may apply to the subjects themselves or to one of their parents.) Generally speaking, these subjects are dignified, grave, prudent and fearless. They are forward-looking and keen on higher education for themselves and others. They can be religious, philosophical and intellectual but they can also be fanatical. They can be tactless or insincere and they may be bullied or oppressed by others.

Saturn in Capricorn

Saturn is the ruler of Capricorn, so its character is at its purest in this sign. Methodical, hard working, disciplined and ambitious, these subjects advance slowly in life and overcome obstacles. At worst, they can be selfish and pessimistic and they may worry unnecessarily over money, but generally these people are sensible, thorough and often successful in business or politics. They have a dry and witty sense of humour.

Saturn in Aquarius

Before the discovery of Uranus, Saturn ruled Aquarius. Its steadying influence and rather serious, intellectual side is helpful in this sign. These subjects are independent, original thinkers who aim high and reach their objectives. They may have scientific or mathematical abilities. If they decide to work for causes, they do so in a thorough manner and they finish what they start. These people are reserved but quite sociable, especially towards their families and their trusted friends. They also have a dry and witty sense of humour. They are forgiving and balanced but also judgemental and somewhat opinionated. They can lead lonely lives.

Saturn in Pisces

This is an excellent placement for workers in the medical profession, teaching or in the church. These subjects are humanitarian, idealistic and romantic and they often implement their socialistic or philosophical beliefs in a practical manner. They can be imaginative but indecisive, moody and manipulative, and their strong emotional nature can be the cause of their undoing. They really do need planets in fixed or Earth signs in order to stabilise their charts.

URANUS

Uranus takes seven years to work its way through a sign and it influences groups of people who were born or raised during a particular time, rather than individuals.

Uranus in Aries

This produces active, freedom-loving, unconventional, positive and independent people who could be inventive engineers or craft workers. There may be unexpected events in life and also the grandparents could be a strong influence.

Uranus in Taurus

These subjects have fixed opinions, and are headstrong, resourceful, disruptive and intense. They attack problems forcefully. They have sudden financial ups and downs and also strange values – possibly anti-materialistic. They may obtain or inherit money from grandparents.

──────────Uranus in Gemini──────────

Versatile, restless, imaginative, nervy, these people may have telepathic ability. They have unusual brothers and sisters or an unusual family situation, as well as an unusual education and possibly an unusual career. Grandparents could have a hand in the subject's education or upbringing.

──────────Uranus in Cancer──────────

These subjects may be emotionally unstable, touchy, eccentric. An original or unusual domestic life may be chosen. They may have had a disrupted childhood, possibly brought up by grandparents.

──────────Uranus in Leo──────────

Hard-working, adventurous, bold, defiant and powerful, these subjects may have interesting children or be interested in child development. They may be domineering and eccentric. Such subjects may have strange grandparents who were a strong influence in childhood.

──────────Uranus in Virgo──────────

There may be an interest in diet and health, cleanliness and alternative therapies. These subjects have good critical faculties and could be inventive teachers. They may be funny about food and they may have strange but rather distant grandparents.

──────────Uranus in Libra──────────

This signifies a dual personality: both charming and disruptive. There is definite evidence of an unusual marriage or partnerships.

They have literary ability and a fondness for television and the media. They are scientific, artistic, and possibly psychic.

——————Uranus in Scorpio——————

These people could have odd ideas about helping others, swinging between being very helpful to being dictatorial or distant. Strange emotional outlets may be needed. These subjects can be independent, determined and emotional but they can also be vindictive and explosive.

——————Uranus in Sagittarius——————

Such subjects can be reckless and independent with some really funny ideas about life. They seek out original forms of study, religion and travel. They may try to put the world to rights. Intuitive, scientific and freedom-loving, these people may well have revolutionary ideas. (This generation could travel in space.)

——————Uranus in Capricorn——————

This group could be keen on politics and may live in a time of powerful political events. With penetrating minds and an authoritative manner, they could be domineering and rebellious or thoughtful and thorough. Highly ambitious.

——————Uranus in Aquarius——————

Resourceful and clever, very intuitive and imaginative, these subjects could be keen on astrology, graphology, numerology, etc. They have original ideas for reform and an interest in science. They are modern thinkers and are humanitarians, but possibly cold and mechanical in outlook, like a totalitarian government.

Uranus in Pisces

This subject is likely to develop or change religious beliefs. Highly intuitive, secretive and emotional with changeable moods, they may have mediumistic dreams. There may be great ups-and-downs in life with scandals and losses being balanced by sudden gains in status and wealth.

NEPTUNE

Neptune spends eleven years in each sign, so its influence is almost generational.

Neptune in Aries

These subjects have unusual personalities. They are emotional, romantic and artistic, and they love to travel. They may be interested in psychic research or some strange form of politics.

Neptune in Taurus

Musical, artistic, creative, these subjects may work in the artistic field. They are likely to suffer from fluctuating finances.

Neptune in Gemini

Such people are mystical, imaginative and prophetic, with many new ideas on religion. They may be peevish and gossipy.

Neptune in Cancer

These subjects are emotional and imaginative. They may choose artistic home surroundings. They love the sea.

Neptune in Leo

There is a terrific interest in glamorous and escapist entertainment. These subjects love the theatre and cinema, and are dramatic, artistic, magnetic and kind.

Neptune in Virgo

Critical of orthodox religion, these subjects are intellectual, intuitive and sensitive. They may suffer from allergies to food and drugs.

Neptune in Libra

This generation grew into the hippies of the 1960s and 1970s. These subjects are gentle, artistic, romantic and keen to find ideal lovers and partners.

Neptune in Scorpio

Extremely sensitive, emotional and, possibly, mediumistic. Secretive, with a strong sense of social justice, these subjects may overturn their parents' social or religious beliefs.

Neptune in Sagittarius

These subjects have a keen love of travel, and may travel through space. New religious ideas may appeal. There is an interest in research, language and literature; however the television/video/ computer age seems to change the influence from writing to visual forms of entertainment and education.

Neptune in Capricorn

This indicates practical ability with business insight, and inspiration which is harnessed to practicality. Changes in religious outlook are likely, possibly indicating a practical attitude to these matters rather than one of blind faith or of psychic or spiritual thought.

Neptune in Aquarius

People with Neptune in Aquarian are likely to involve themselves in a search for new religious ideas. Humanitarianism and independence are of great importance, as are new romantic ideas and a new social order.

Neptune in Pisces

Mysterious religions are signified here. This generation may reach the heights or sink into the depths. Allergies and strange ailments may abound.

PLUTO

Pluto has a very eccentric orbit which means that it can stay for as little as thirteen years in a sign or as long as thirty-three years. It is truly a generational influence.

Pluto in Gemini (1900 to 1914)

A time of scientific discoveries. This generation witnessed the rise of socialism, and trades unions. There was universal education in Europe and America.

Pluto in Cancer (1914 to 1939)

This generation is influenced by the two world wars. Homes and families were broken up by wars. Time was spent in the armed services. There was a rise in council house building and a strong government influence in ordinary people's lives.

Pluto in Leo (1939 to 1958)

These were the war years and the austerity years. It was a time of transformation of the ruling classes, the rise of mass media and new ideas on education and child welfare.

Pluto in Virgo (1958 to 1971)

Changes in social and sexual rules. Improvements in health and mass living and working conditions. Analytical attitude to world problems. Television age and beginnings of space exploration.

Pluto in Libra (1971 to 1983)

This time saw changes in methods of business, marriage and family life. People were striving to eliminate world wars and the nuclear threat in the interest of a partnership between nature and man. These years introduced the beginnings of a real interest in ecology.

Pluto in Scorpio (1983 to 1995)

The Soviet Union ended, bringing changes in power blocks. There has been a reduction of nuclear arms and some conventional arms but changes in power bases. This period has also witnessed the rise of AIDS (could this problem be solved when Pluto leaves Scorpio?). We are starting to see the results of changes in family structures and there have been even more changes in the way society and the family is arranged. There has been a rise in criminality and terrorism, as well as changes in the coal, oil, gas and diamond industries.

Pluto in Sagittarius (1995 onwards)

We will have to wait and see!

CHIRON

It would be nice to include the asteroid, Chiron, in this book but there isn't much known about it yet. However, a friend of mine called Anne Christie has done quite a bit of research on this which has led me to look into it too. These are the conclusions that Anne and I have come to.

Chiron has a slightly eccentric orbit, but it takes from about two to three years to traverse a sign. Anne and I have concluded that, in a natal chart, Chiron points out health weaknesses and other problems which have to be surmounted. It points to times of crisis by progression or transit or when being crossed by some other planet. The problems which show up when Chiron hits a soft spot are often health-related and even when they are not, the stress invariably brings a health problem in its wake. In a natal chart, it is worth looking at the sign that Chiron occupies, the one it opposes, its house, the opposite house, as well as any aspects to the planets and angles. Please excuse me if I use the examples which I have readily to hand which, of course, are from my own household.

My own Chiron is at two degrees of Virgo in the fourth house. It opposes Pisces and the tenth house and it is in a wide square to Uranus which is at eight degrees of Gemini. My own health has never been good and my family have had their share of severe health problems. The need to conserve my own strength and to be on hand for the family has been instrumental in my choice of career as an astrologer. I have used the knowledge I have gained from learning about astrology, psychology and spiritual healing in addition to living through difficulties myself in order to help others. Virgo is all about health and healing and Pisces is spiritual and mystic. The fourth house is concerned with family matters and the tenth house is career-orientated. My childhood was made difficult by the sudden death of my father and my mother's need to concentrate on taking over his engineering business. (Fourth and tenth – parents. Uranus – sudden catastrophe.) I was brought up and strongly influenced by my grandparents, especially my grandmother. (Uranus – grandparents, especially grandmother.)

There have subsequently been many emergencies and problems to cope with in the family and it is usually me at the sharp end of them.

Here is a good example of a Chiron transit. A couple of years ago, I came in from a trip to the supermarket to find my husband, Tony, writhing in agony and vomiting all over the place. Thank goodness the problem turned out to be a kidney stone which, mercifully, passed after he got to hospital. Chiron, which was in Leo at the time, was making a nasty 'T square' to his Sun/Mercury conjunction in Scorpio and his Moon in Taurus. The mental picture of an ambulance in front of the house and all the neighbours hanging out of their windows to see what is going on is a wonderful visual archetype for a Chiron transit!

Well, we need more than a handful of charts before making any real judgement, so we must all look at Chiron against as many charts as we can in order to gain some real insight. It does seem to be important, that's for sure.

CHAPTER 7

Angles, Hemispheres, Elements and Qualities

The Ascendant, Nadir, Descendant and Midheaven

The Ascendant, Often Referred to as the ASC

The ascendant is the exact degree of the sign of the zodiac which is coming up over the horizon when a new baby makes his first cry, or at the exact moment when an enterprise begins. (If you want to know more about this area of astrology, read my book *Rising Signs* which goes into it in depth.)

If a subject is born at dawn his Sun will be on the ascendant; if he is born at dusk it will be on the descendant; if at noon, it will be on the midheaven; and if at midnight it will be on the nadir.

The ascendant has a bearing on a subject's outer manner, his appearance and the way he lives. It may determine the kind of career he takes up. The ascendant is linked to the first house of the *self*, the body and the subject's personal manner. Nothing is cut and dried in astrology, but the ascendant is a strong modifying factor on anybody's chart and is sometimes more obvious than the Sun sign. Planets which are close to the ascendant have a very strong effect on the subject's personality and lifestyle.

The Nadir, Also Known as the Immum Coeli or IC

In any system other than the equal house system, this is the cusp of the fourth house. Depending on how the chart is arranged, it can be found at or near the bottom of the birthchart. This relates to a subject's home and domestic circumstances. It also relates to the circumstances which prevailed at the beginning of his life and which might occur at the end of his life. It may throw some light

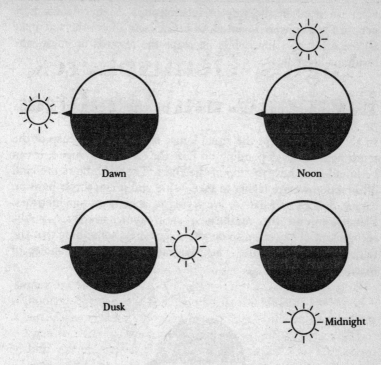

Figure 1 The Sun's passage in relation to the horizon (▲)

on his relationship with his parents, especially his mother. Planets around the IC show an intense need for financial and emotional security.

The Descendant, Also Known as the DSC

In all systems, including the equal house system, this is the cusp of the seventh house and it is always found opposite the ascendant. We tend to choose people as partners, lovers and colleagues who have the kind of character and values which can be found in the sign on the descendant. Planets which are close to the descendant can show the influence that others have on us or they can show what we need in the way of relationships. Many planets here denote a person who is content to sit back and allow others to make all the effort for him, while he reaps the rewards or enjoys the resultant lifestyle.

The Midheaven, Also Known as the Medium Coeli or MC

In all systems, except the equal house one, this is the cusp of the tenth house and, depending on how the chart is arranged, it can be found at or near the top of the chart. The MC shows the kind of direction we are trying to take in life and it can throw light on career choices or what we are trying to achieve in our lifetimes. Planets around the midheaven show some need for public recognition. They can also denote a search for something that the father failed to provide. The MC can also show the choice of marriage partner.

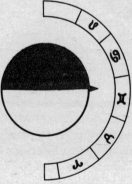

Figure 2   The signs of the zodiac rising up over the ecliptic.
In this case the rising sign is Gemini.

——Hemispheres, Elements and Qualities——

The basic information in this section is similar to that in my book *Understanding Astrology* but I have expanded it with a few suggestions which may help beginners. For example, be careful with the section on hemispheres which follows this. It is all standard astrological theory but it needs to be looked at carefully and not swallowed whole without some thought! For example, a stacked upper hemisphere does not necessarily mean that the subject leads a very public life, nor does a stacked lower hemisphere necessarily imply that he leads a very private life. Read the theory, look at a good few charts and do some research for yourself, so that you can see what fits and what doesn't.

Hemispheres

A birthchart is like looking *southwards* at a map of the sky. If you think about it, from a northern hemisphere country such as Great Britain, the Sun is always to the south of us. East on a birthchart is where west would be on a map of the world. If this confuses you, just don't think about it. Astrology is astrology and geography is geography!

THE UPPER (SOUTHERN) HEMISPHERE

The upper hemisphere contains the 7th, 8th, 9th, 10th, 11th and 12th houses. A subject with most of his planets in this part of his chart will not necessarily be too deeply affected by the actions of other people. He will be able to distance himself from those around him and also from public movements and events. He may keep his eye firmly fixed on the main chance, or on his own needs and feelings, or on the needs of humanity in general, rather than spend his energies on those who are around him. Such a person has a need to develop a career or a personal philosophy of life which fulfils him. If the planets are grouped in the 8th, 9th or 12th houses, the subject will have strong spiritual needs and will see life in terms of related spiritual values. If they are in the 10th, he will be ambitious and politically astute, while if they are in the 11th, he will be interested in humanity in general and education in particular.

THE LOWER (NORTHERN) HEMISPHERE

The lower hemisphere contains the 1st, 2nd, 3rd, 4th, 5th and 6th houses. A subject who has most of his planets in this part of the

chart will be sensitive to the moods and feelings of those around
him and may suffer a good deal as a result. He may try to live
through his family rather than for himself, he may be too
subjective, or he may simply choose to do most of his thinking and
working at home.

THE EASTERN HEMISPHERE
The eastern hemisphere contains the 10th, 11th, 12th, 1st, 2nd and
3rd houses. A subject who has most of his planets in this area of
the chart is a self-starter who chooses his own path through life
and sets his own boundaries. He is not happy living off other
people or being kept by someone else. He has the burden of being
an initiator both at work and in his personal life, as little is likely
to be done for him by others. When the planets are in the first
three houses, the subject is very self-absorbed and convinced that
his own opinions are the only ones which matter.

THE WESTERN HEMISPHERE
The western hemisphere contains the 4th, 5th, 6th, 7th, 8th and
9th houses. A subject who has most of his planets in this area of
the chart will need to be very diplomatic in order to keep those
around him on his side. He may be looked after in some way by
other people or he may spend his life supporting and motivating
others. When the majority of planets are in the 6th, 7th and 8th
houses, he will use his energy to fulfil the needs of others. He may
create a situation of being needed by bringing a number of children
into the world to love and look after.

The Elements

FIRE
The key ideas here are of enthusiasm, initiative, intuition,
optimism and faith in the future. Fiery people never quite
relinquish their childhood and are, therefore, in tune with young
people and young ideas. These entertaining people display
considerable egotism but also spontaneous generosity. They get

things started, create action and pace but they may leave the details to others to cope with. Fire sign people are quick to grasp an idea and, 'being on the ball', they approach life with a degree of sportsmanship as if it were a kind of game. These people find it difficult to save money but they can usually earn their way out of disaster. Fire subjects have very hot tempers but, once they have shouted and raved a little, the steam goes out of them and they settle back into their usual good-humoured nature once again. Ariens and Sagittarians don't hold grudges but Leos do.

EARTH

This element is concerned with security, structure, slow growth, conventional behaviour and concrete results. Earth people are sensible, possibly rather plodding and very practical in outlook. They do things thoroughly and carefully, they are unlikely to be extravagant and are very caring towards their family and close friends. They hold on to their possessions and may be a little too money-minded at times. They hate to give up anything and will always try to finish any job that they start. There is a sense of maturity with these people but perhaps a lack of spontaneity. Their virtue is their reliability while their vices are fussiness and an 'eye-on-the-main-chance' attitude. Earth people are slow to rouse to anger but they don't cool down again for a long time once they are roused. Fire and air people can find Earth sign people boring.

AIR

This element is concerned with communications, networks of all kinds, education, theoretical ideas, finding answers to questions and all-round enlightenment. These subjects may be serious-minded and highly involved with the education system, or they can be chirpy, streetwise people who pick up the latest information on the airwaves. They can be found expounding on a pet idea, or arguing a point over anything from a literary reference to a sporting event. They make good journalists and shopkeepers, teachers and travellers because they are always up to date. Although kind-hearted, they tend to forget their many friends when out of sight. They are not especially hot-tempered but they can become extremely angry over an injustice. Earth and water people can find Geminis and Librans too flighty.

WATER
This element is concerned with emotions, feelings, inner moods and urges. Watery people respond slowly when asked a question and they may appear slow when grasping a new concept. However, they are not slow or stupid, it's just that they need time for everything to filter through their highly intuitive aura before it hits the brain. Water people are slow to change, preferring to stay on a tried and tested path. Their chief need is to be close to their family and also to have financial security. However, Pisces is less concerned with either family or security than Scorpio or Cancer. Faithful, loyal and rather tense, water people have an intuitive feeling for what is right for themselves and their families. They are usually sensible and reliable but if their feelings are stirred up, they can react strangely. They can become depressed and ill if they are not loved enough. Water people are very sympathetic to the needs of others and they often choose to work in jobs which help others. Most water people appreciate artistic or creative matters, with music being the absolute favourite. These people don't lose their temper easily but they can be very destructive to themselves or others when they do. Scorpio can be extremely destructive, sometimes for no real reason.

The Qualities

Cardinal
After many years as a professional astrologer, I am not sure that cardinal people are the great initiators or pioneers that they are supposed to be. Ariens and Capricornians like being part of a large organisation, while Librans and Cancerians enjoy being part of a group. These subjects don't seem to enjoy taking independent decisions and they function best as part of a team. They have the energy and determination to succeed but they don't want to be the

first to do anything new, to go out on a limb or to take totally independent action. All these signs are ambitious. Cancerians and Librans are both personally ambitious and also ambitious for their families, while Ariens and Capricornians may be keen on promoting their organisation as well as themselves and their families. There is a dynastic feel to all these signs and, once they have found the right avenue for their talents, they go as far as they can.

Fixed

The usual astrological description of these people seems to be about right. Fixed people don't like change. They stick to their jobs, homes and families through thick and thin and they have the strength and determination to see things through or to hold up the status quo. They may stick in a bad job or a bad relationship too long and they may fear change. These subjects are all stubborn and determined and they work hard to have and to hold.

Mutable

Once again, I feel that 'received' astrological wisdom is wrong here. Mutable people are supposed to hang on to outworn lifestyles and to resist change but this is simply not so. Mutable people have the courage to take their own, very independent path and to do the things that nobody has done before. These subjects are the bungee jumpers of the zodiac who launch themselves over the edge with a kind of crazy faith in their guardian angels. Mutable subjects are adaptable and they will fit in with most situations and most types of people. They try to find some point of contact or understanding between themselves and even the oddest people. Their thinking is wider and more lateral than the other two types and their friendliness and good humour lead them to enjoy and to see the funny side of even the nastiest situations. They suffer from boredom and may be addicted to travel, new faces, change and simply being different. People who have strongly mutable charts tend to go through life feeling alone or lonely.

Masculine and Feminine – Positive and Negative

Every alternate sign is masculine/positive or feminine/negative.
The theory is that the masculine signs are the confident go-getters
while the feminine ones are weak, moody and lacking in assertion.
This theory works reasonably well but it is a bit too black and white
for comfort.

The Missing Link

It is always worth looking around the chart to see what is missing.
For instance, does the chart lack water? Are there no planets in
fixed signs? Is there a lack of femininity or are there any
unaspected planets? Are there any intercepted signs or any
segments of the chart with nothing going on? Some people
compensate for their missing factors while others live without ever
bothering with them.

CHAPTER 8
The Houses

The Great House Controversy

There are twelve houses on a birthchart. These start at the ascendant and work their way round the chart. There are many house systems to choose from and each astrologer has to find the one that suits him best. An astrologer may stick to the system he first learned or he may decide that another one 'feels' right later on. This is all entirely subjective.

When I first learned astrology I used the equal house system. There were no computer programs in those days and all charts had to be made up by hand. The equal house method was quicker to work out than any other and it was less inclined to allow inaccuracies to creep in. I began to switch to the Placidus system when I started to use computers. The program which I use now expresses the signs and houses by keeping the signs equal and squashing up or spreading out the houses across them. This is easy to use because the angles between the planets are easy to spot. I occasionally use the topocentric system for a change; this is a slight variation on the Placidus system. Many people now use the Koch system which is favoured by Bruno and Louise Huber, and in France, I gather that the Campanus system is popular.

The Houses

Each planet is connected to a sign and a house which have similar characteristics. The connections between the signs, houses and planets are as follows:

Sign	*House*	*Planet*
Aries	First	Mars
Taurus	Second	Venus
Gemini	Third	Mercury
Cancer	Fourth	Moon
Leo	Fifth	Sun
Virgo	Sixth	Mercury
Libra	Seventh	Venus
Scorpio	Eighth	Pluto (also Mars)
Sagittarius	Ninth	Jupiter
Capricorn	Tenth	Saturn
Aquarius	Eleventh	Uranus (also Saturn)
Pisces	Twelfth	Neptune (also Jupiter)

If you bear in mind that astrology is a kind of permutation between these energies which are repeated over and again in the form of the planets, modified by the signs and used according to the houses they occupy, you will have grasped the essentials and will be halfway to being able to zip through chart interpretation in record speed.

————A Brief Introduction to the Houses————

If the ascendant falls near the beginning of a sign, that sign will occupy most of the first house. If it falls towards the end of a sign, then there will be a little bit of the sign which the ascendant crosses, plus a lot of the next sign in the first house. The shape, size and occupancy of houses can be further complicated by using any house system other than the equal house type.

The following is a brief introduction to the houses but you can extend your knowledge by re-reading the earlier sections in this book which relate to the planets and the signs but *this time*, using the information in order to enhance your knowledge of the houses. For example, a clearer idea of Venus and Taurus will tell you more about the second house, while a delve into Uranus and Aquarius will tell you more about the eleventh house.

The First House
This is similar to Aries and Mars and it is an *angular* house.

Many people are more like their rising sign or first house, than their Sun sign. In some cases, this represents an outward appearance which is different from the main part of a person's character while, in other cases, the subject is exactly like his Sun sign but has traits which belong to the rising sign and the first house. Unfortunately there are no hard and fast rules and one has to approach each chart with an open mind. My own family is a wonderful example to study. In my immediate family, we have six Leos, four Scorpios and three Taureans. Each one of us has variations on a theme and it is fascinating to see the similarities and the differences between each group.

Traditionally, therefore, the first house should rule the subject's looks, outer manner and some aspects of health. It may throw light on his family background and the way he was treated or taught as a child. His behaviour and manner may be the result of his background and upbringing but, astrology being what it is, his manner and behaviour may be all his own invention. This house, like the Sun sign, represents aspects of the self. It can show how he approaches life, the career he chooses or where he directs his energies. One thing for sure, any planets which are found in this house are likely to have a strong influence.

The Second House
This is similar to Taurus and Venus and it is a *succedent* house. It is concerned with personal possessions and personal finances, and basic needs such as food, clothing and shelter. It is also concerned with values, priorities and self-esteem, some aspects of the feelings and of relationships, and the five senses.

The Third House
This is similar to Gemini and Mercury and it is a *cadent* house. It rules brothers and sisters, cousins and other relatives of one's own generation. Also neighbours and local matters. Traditionally,

it concerns local travel and short journeys but this could now be extended into any kind of travel which is normal for the subject. It also rules communications and information of all kinds, paperwork and negotiations of all kinds, and education, but not usually higher education. The capacity to think and the way a subject expresses himself are indicated by this house, as are dexterity and figure work.

The Fourth House

This is similar to Cancer and the Moon and it is an *angular* house. In all but the equal house system, this starts at the IC (immum coeli or nadir). This rules the parents; traditionally, the mother figure or the person who nurtured the subject. It concerns the childhood home and domestic circumstances throughout life, as well as land or property matters. Traditionally, it represents the beginning and the end of life.

The Fifth House

Similar to Leo and the Sun, this is a *succedent* house. It rules anything that the subject creates. This covers artistry and creativity, especially music; the creation of a family, especially children; pleasures, holidays and hobbies which are fun or amusing; love affairs and any spontaneous affection such as that for pets, small children, and so on. It also rules time off from the struggle of daily life.

The Sixth House

Similar to Virgo and Mercury, this is a *cadent* house. Traditionally, it is the house of employers and employees, so it has much to do with work and duty. This house also rules health and prevention of illness, food and the harvest, and duties to others.

The Seventh House

Similar to Libra and Venus this is an *angular* house which starts at the descendant. It rules aboveboard relationships, traditionally marriage, as well as colleagues, business partners, close friends and even open enemies. The seventh house also concerns agreements, especially legal ones, and justice, whether of the legal and official kind or of the more casual kind.

The Eighth House

Similar to Scorpio and Pluto this is a *succedent* house which rules committed relationships. It also concerns shared finances and resources, your partner's finances or resources, dealings with large financial institutions, legacies, taxes, corporate matters, and the financial side of any partnership. This house also rules birth, death, beginnings and endings, sex, karma — what you give out and how it comes back — one's approach to birth and death and the afterlife, and occult or hidden matters both of the mystical and non-mystical kind. Another area ruled by this house is dealings with the police, etc.

The Ninth House

Similar to Sagittarius and Jupiter this is a *cadent* house ruling foreign travel, especially exploration and expeditions of one kind or another, foreigners, and freedom and independence. The legal profession, religion and philosophical matters, higher education, and pushing back boundaries are also incorporated into this house.

The Tenth House

Similar to Capricorn and Saturn this is an *angular* house. In all but the equal house system, this starts at the M.C. (medium coeli or midheaven). This rules the aims, ambitions, direction in life: what one is striving to achieve in this lifetime. Parents, especially father figures or those who exerted discipline, are concerned, as are work, career, status and standing, public acclaim outside the

home and the subject's immediate circle, achievements, responsibilities and one's public image. This also rules circumstances
which, depending upon other factors, can bring limitations or
opportunities.

The Eleventh House
Similar to Aquarius and Uranus this is a *succedent* house ruling
friends and acquaintances, and detached or more distant
relationships. Education and the aquisition of knowledge. It also
concerns group activities such as clubs, societies, unions,
workshops and so on, intellectual pleasures such as crosswords,
etc., astrology, and hopes and wishes.

The Twelfth House
Similar to Neptune and Pisces this is a *cadent* house which rules
service to others, self-sacrifice and caring for the weak. It also
concerns self-undoing, escapism, the mystical side of life and the
occult, the unconscious and, therefore, deeply hidden urges or
needs. It denotes sensitivity, creativity and artistry.

───────────Ancient Houses───────────
My friend, Jonathan Dee has dredged up the following fascinating
information. The lists show the way that various astrologers across
the centuries have viewed the astrological houses. It is interesting
to see the differences in thinking over such long periods of time,
but it is even more interesting to see the similarities!

─────── The Vedic houses (long ───────
before the birth of Christ)

The Houses	The Interpretations
First	The appearance
Second	Inheritance and wealth
Third	Bad luck
Fourth	The mother

Fifth	The mind, intellect, memory
Sixth	Enemies
Seventh	Death of the wife
Eighth	Death and losses
Ninth	Good luck
Tenth	The father and journeys
Eleventh	Personal gains
Twelfth	Costs and bondage

─────────Ptolemy (150 BC)─────────

The Houses	The Interpretations
First	Horoscopus — the hour
Second	The gate of Hades (Pluto = wealth)
Third	Dedicated to the goddess (Isis)
Fourth	Immum coeli
Fifth	Fortuna major
Sixth	Bad fortune
Seventh	Occidentos (the west)
Eighth	Illness and the beginning of death
Ninth	God
Tenth	Medium coeli
Eleventh	Good daemon (good spirit who looks after one)
Twelfth	Bad daemon (bad spirit)

─────────Firmicus Maternus (AD 400)─────────

Jonathan and I translated this between us, hopefully earning us both some Brownie points.

The Houses	The Interpretations	Translation
First	Vita	Life
Second	Lucrum	Money, possessions
Third	Fractres	Brothers, brotherhood
Fourth	Domus (genitor)	Home (heredity)
Fifth	File (nati)	Son (children)
Sixth	Valetudo	Health

Seventh	Uxor	The wife
Eighth	Mors	Death
Ninth	Philosophia (pietas)	Belief (piety)
Tenth	Patres (regnum)	The father (ruler, reign)
Eleventh	Fortuna (benefactum)	Good fortune, benefit
Twelfth	Carcer	Incarceration

——————William Lilly (AD 1647)——————

The Houses	The Interpretations
First	Life of man, stature and colour
Second	State, fortune, wealth, in-laws
Third	Brethren, letters, neighbours
Fourth	Father, lands, end of life
Fifth	Children, amour, plays, conceits, ambassadors
Sixth	Sickness, servants, uncles (paternal, cattle)
Seventh	Marriage, alliances, enemies, duels, lawsuits
Eighth	Death, estates, wills
Ninth	Voyages, learning, visions and dreams
Tenth	Royalty, mother, honour, authorities
Eleventh	Friends, courtiers, hope and confidence
Twelfth	Intrigue, private enemies, secrets, prison

——————Conrad Ebertine (AD 1940)——————

The Houses	The Interpretations
First	Personality, childhood
Second	Material foundations of life
Third	Relationships in the immediate environment
Fourth	Parental home and heredity
Fifth	Assurance of progeny through the sex urge
Sixth	Work, teamwork, co-operation
Seventh	Union, partnership, marriage
Eighth	Birth and death
Ninth	Spiritual life, religion
Tenth	Aims, vocation, old age, struggle

| Eleventh | Wishes, hopes, ties through friendship |
| Twelfth | Seclusion, solitude, the close of life |

—————————Jeff Mayo (AD 1964)—————————

The Houses	The Interpretations
First	Self-centred interests
Second	Possessions, personal security
Third	Relationship to the environment
Fourth	Beginnings, possessions, relatives
Fifth	Recreation, self-expression
Sixth	Service to the community, health
Seventh	Personal identity with others
Eighth	Sacrifice, shared resources
Ninth	New horizons
Tenth	Status, material responsibility
Eleventh	Group identification
Twelfth	Self-sacrifice, escapism, confinement

CHAPTER 9

Planets in Houses

The planets don't work in quite the same way in the houses as they do in the signs. The sign modifies the character of the planet but the house shows *how it is used*. For example, *Mercury in Virgo* is analytical in character and when in the *second house*, this would be used to gain wealth or to conserve something. This person could, therefore, be a farmer who plays the stock market in his spare time!

The Sun

First These subjects are concerned with themselves and the projection of their personalities. They can be self-centred.

Second Centred on financial matters or keen on possessions. These subjects may be materialistic or they may simply want a comfortable life. They have a high earning capacity and can be possessive over goods or people. They are cautious over decisions and they usually seek harmonious relationships with others.

Third Fluent talkers who need to communicate. They may work in journalism, the media, teaching or writing, or they may deal with neighbourhood matters. These people can be closely attached to sisters, brothers and cousins. They can lack patience and consistency.

Fourth These subjects are interested in home and family and they will help family members. They are conscious of background and family history and may take up genealogy or history as a hobby. They may be collectors.

Many choose to work from home. They have a caring personality but they can be shy or withdrawn. Some of them lose out on parental love in childhood. Excellent listeners.

Fifth These subjects can be over-generous. They need to enjoy life to the full but may want more than is possible. They are very fond of children. They may be musical, creative or sporty. Some have many love affairs while others are unusually faithful to one partner. Stubborn. They are drawn to showbiz and glamorous professions.

Sixth Hardworking with good organising ability and a head for details but forgetful about things that don't interest them. These people are health conscious and they can be hypochondriacs. They can be difficult and exacting, and they are better talkers than listeners.

Seventh These subjects want to be liked. They enjoy marriage and working partnerships. They want to express themselves but they may have to do what others dictate. These subjects may be lazy or prefer to lean on others who make decisions for them. Good looking, musical, creative, popular.

Eighth Interested in the afterlife, possibly involved in deeds, wills and official matters related to life and death. These subjects can be interested in medicine, forensic investigation, detective work or the occult. These people have powerful but difficult personalities. They may be involved with other people's finances.

Ninth Many of these subjects choose to live in different countries from those in which they grew up. They are tolerant of different cultures and they may have a flair for languages. Broadminded outlook. They may be attracted to religion, education or the law. Some choose to work with animals, while others become involved in publishing or broadcasting.

Tenth Interested in career, status, advancement, politics and public image. They may have a vocation which causes them to neglect family and friends.

Hardworking, dedicated and somewhat austere.

Eleventh May officiate in clubs and societies or work for the betterment of humanity. Friendly and open-minded, they try to make others happy. They can be detached in personal relationships and not particularly fond of family life.

Twelfth These subjects like to work alone and they may also choose to live alone. They are very sensitive and introverted. These people need their own home comforts and, if they must have people around them, they choose people they know well and whom they can trust. They may be interested in art, music and creative pursuits and they may want to escape from reality from time to time. These people are interested in the occult and they may be quite clairvoyant. They may have hidden sides to their personality which only come out after living or working with them for a while.

The Moon

First These subjects are strongly affected by their mothers and the relationship is either very good or pretty awful, but it always has an unforgettable impact. The emotions are strong and the subject is sensitive, but the feelings and emotions can be suppressed, especially in males. These people can take their anguish out on a partner, making them pay for a parent's sins. Others try to heal the world or put the environment to rights rather than concentrate on developing personal relationships. The damage which may be done in childhood and any difficult behaviour patterns that are carried forward into adult life may be eased if the Moon is in a feminine sign or if it is well-aspected.

The sign which is rising is strongly emphasised and the effects of the Moon will be coloured by whatever sign is involved. Those who have the Moon in the first house are restless, they are fond of travel and the sea. Some need a certain amount of their own company while others cling to their families.

Second   These subjects need security and they may save or collect goods, money or antiques. They may simply surround themselves with clutter in order to feel safe and secure. These people have good business instincts but their income or their luck can ebb and flow, like the tides. Their feelings towards their loved ones are very strong and they can be possessive.

Third   Attached to their siblings or to a neighbourhood that they know well. They may take responsibility for other family members. Their early education is unsettled, and they may never really find it easy to concentrate or to stick to one idea.

Fourth · Clinging, maternal and homeloving. Some of these subjects demand more love and affection than anyone can reasonably give them. They may try to cling to old lovers, children, friends and their past. They are loyal to their family and friends. These people may be interested in history or objects which have a 'provenance'. Some of these subjects choose to work from home, or to work with children in a family atmosphere.

Fifth   Outgoing and rather dramatic in their approach to love and life. They may be attracted to a glamorous lifestyle, possibly in the world of the arts, the stage or sports. Alternatively, they might fill their homes and their lives with children. They may marry someone who has children or they may teach.

Sixth   These subjects may have been ailing in childhood, or they may be obsessed by health, hygiene or food. They may work from home, bring work home or move their homes due to work. They may have a demanding mother or they may, in turn, be a demanding or exacting parent. The may have to cope with a chronic illness.

Seventh   May be vulnerable and dependent, needing a maternal partner, but they can also seek to smother or control others. They are very interested in business matters and they make successful working partnerships.

Eighth   Interested in psychic or intuitive subjects with strong powers of ESP. They may be preoccupied with life and death and the spiritual side of things. Sex is another strong interest for these subjects. These people may become involved in public finances or they may be strongly influenced by a partner's financial position. They have a talent for business and can be extremely successful in business partnerships or even as lone entrepreneurs.

Ninth   Attracted to spiritual subjects, may pursue an interest in a variety of esoteric interests. They may be keen on languages. They usually travel a good deal and they may choose to live or work in a different country from the one in which they grew up. Some marry foreigners. Many interests, including such things as ecology, animals, legal matters and politics. They may write or broadcast.

Tenth   These subjects take their careers very seriously and this can take precedence over their private lives. They may be drawn to politics or public service of some kind. They may achieve wealth or fame, although this can be at the cost of their family life. Their families may be drawn into their public worlds (such as a politician's husband or wife).

Eleventh   These subjects may be cool or detached. They are keen on friends, clubs and group activities, but they may be uninterested in family life. Some are happier at work than at home. Their objectives are changeable and their interests varied. They have many friends and acquaintances.

Twelfth   These subjects need time (sometimes years) in order to cope with their childhoods and their feelings towards parents, previous spouses or other members of their families. They may learn hard lessons through relatives. They appear tough but they are very soft inside and they are easily hurt. In some cases, the proximity of the Moon to the ascendant makes these subjects similar to those who have the Moon in the first house. There is often some kind of hidden and unresolved problem which has been left over from the subject's childhood. This suppressed pain and rage may erupt in an inappropriate manner later in life or it may result in strange behaviour when the subject is under stress.

Mercury

First These subjects may be very clever and literate or they may find thinking, talking or writing difficult. The same applies to numeracy, e.g. they could be computer and accounts wizards or, conversely, unable to cope with numbers. They try to make an intellectual impact on the world. Some overrule feelings with logic. Their thinking may be too diverse or too self-centred.

Second Businesslike and business-minded. Possibly large scale wheeler-dealers. Practical and dexterous. Good craftsmen or musicians. Interested in food and cookery.

Third Keen on education, good teachers. They may be closely involved with brothers and sisters, neighbours or neighbourhood matters. Local travel and vehicles could figure strongly in their lives. They may release pent up tension by writing poetry or music.

Fourth These subjects are fond of their home surroundings and they may choose to work from home. Maternal and domesticated, they make a point of talking and listening to their children and they are also keen on educating them. These people may be interested in history or collecting things which have a past. They can work from home as counsellors or 'agony aunts' (or astrologers)!

Fifth May teach or be intellectually involved with children.

Good at intellectual games but may be easily bored by work which requires attention to detail or a rigid routine. They want both love and sex, and they see sex as an essential part of communication. They also need a lover with whom they can really talk.

Sixth   These subjects have very analytical minds and they make excellent secretaries. They can be academic, musical or good at craft and design. They may be nervous, fussy or health-conscious. They find it hard to plan or to look forward with optimism, and they may suffer from a low sense of self-esteem. Some talk incessantly about nothing.

Seventh   These subjects seek an intellectual rapport with others. They are good friends and also excellent diplomats or liaison officers. They have a good attitude to marriage and working partnerships. They may be better talkers than listeners. Some are excellent designers or craftsmen. If Mercury is afflicted, these subjects may be prone to illness.

Eighth   Clever businessmen and women who have clever ideas. They are deep thinkers. They may be interested in the occult, religion and the afterlife. They may be keen on reading or writing thrillers or working in the undertaking industry. Their emotions are deep but they may be expressed in an intellectual manner. They have good concentration but an afflicted Mercury can cause blockages in the thinking processes.

Ninth   Good students and teachers with a flair for English or foreign languages. They may have too many ideas to bring any of them to fruition and they need to apply themselves conscientiously.

Tenth   Can be drawn to a career in communications or a business which has a communicative basis. They need a mental outlet or they can become unhappy or frustrated.

Eleventh   These subjects enjoy being involved with clubs and societies and they have many friends. They are approachable and friendly, although they can be sarcastic and tactless at times. They have wide-ranging ideas about politics.

Twelfth   Inward-looking and secretive, their inner feelings are very important to them. They are sensitive, thoughtful and kind. Some are attracted to mysticism and they may write or compose music on these themes. These people may have problems in connection with their work or their health and they need a happy and stable marriage in order to function successfully.

Venus

First   Good looking. This is a good placement for models, starlets or work in the fashion or glamour industry. Interested in art, music and things of beauty. They enjoy flattery. They enjoy luxury and can be sybaritic or lazy.

Second   Could collect or create attractive and valuable artefacts. Could be interested in the arts or the business side of art or beauty. Clever business people, probably materialistic. May be interested in craft work, cookery, gardening. Sensual.

Third   Sociable and friendly. They get on well with siblings and relatives and neighbours. Could attract wealthy or influential friends or colleagues. Can study successfully, especially if the chosen subject has an artistic, musical, cultural or beauty bias. Could be extravagant, especially where the family is concerned. Could collect valuable items of an intellectual nature, such as books. They make good agents or liaison officers.

Fourth   These subjects make beautiful homes with lovely decor, flower arrangements, etc. Could be extravagant, especially where the family is concerned. Could be successful antique collectors or dealers. Could succeed in the fields of insurance, property, shop-keeping. Could have wealthy parents, especially the mother.

Fifth	Children liked, may work with them in some way. These subjects' children should turn out rich or successful in some glamorous industry. Love of glamour and the fun side of life. Could enjoy flirtation, love affairs, travel, games, sports, gambling and all kinds of amusements and treats. May be very creative and artistic, also fond of music. Could have very creative children.
Sixth	These subjects need to work in pleasant surroundings with good working conditions. May choose a glamorous career. They dislike hard physical or dirty work. May be health-conscious but basically strong unless Venus is afflicted. Will gain money and influence through work.
Seventh	These people could marry for money. If they marry for love, they could still find themselves in easy circumstances as a result. Good placement for a happy marriage or for marriage to a successful partner (not always the same thing!). Affectionate, loving but needing validation and encouragement from others.
Eighth	Very intense and rather jealous feelings. Could be strongly-sexed or not interested in sex. May inherit (or marry) money. Could make career out of the police, medical, or some other kind of diagnostic or investigative work (Dynorod?).
Ninth	These subjects could do well at school or university. May marry foreigners. May make money from the travel trade in some way. Could travel for fun. May inherit money or obtain it through a second marriage or through in-laws. Could become happily involved in spiritual or religious matters, possibly through marriage. May make a career in the law, arbitration or liaison work.
Tenth	These subjects should have happy and successful careers, especially in something which makes money and also brings them fame. Could work in a feminine or glamour career. Good manner with people,

especially in business. Could do well or make money by being associated with influential people.

Eleventh   Diplomatic and good with people. Discreet. Could be happy working for clubs, societies or with groups of people. Clever politicians. Could have rich or influential friends.

Twelfth   Attracted to the occult or to mysticism. May have secret love affairs or secret vices! A need for seclusion and time to oneself. Creative, imaginative, artistic, musical.

Mars

First   These subjects have assertive personalities and they may be pushy, domineering and difficult. Alternatively, the Mars energy can be channelled into sport, adventure, the military life, pioneering or exploration. They may be impulsive, reckless and full of daring. These people can be very highly-sexed, and sex will always play a strong part in their lives. These subjects can have red hair and a hot temper to go with it. Alternatively, they may have a mole, wart, strawberry or other mark on the head or face. They can suffer from headaches, head injuries or high blood-pressure.

Second   Aggressive money-makers who are competitive in business or in any sphere where land, possessions and money are concerned. They may have wonderful singing voices or simply loud voices which they use to dominate a conversation. These subjects can be high earners but they can also be extravagant. These people are strongly sensual and they may be able to release their tensions through great lovemaking. The throat is sensitive.

Third   These subjects could be keen students both at school and later in life, they have quick and active minds. These people are protective towards their families and, either especially close to, or antagonistic towards their siblings. They can be argumentative or verbally aggressive. Alternatively, they may use words purposefully as part of a job, for instance as a writer, broadcaster or salesperson. Sexual matters must have a strong intellectual feel to them and these subjects are unlikely to be attracted to a slow or stupid partner. The arms, shoulders, wrists and hands are weak points, as are the lungs.

Fourth   These subjects work hard in the home and are very attached to their homes and families. This placement can be a considerably softening factor in a hard and aggressive chart but it can be the worst thing in the world in a soft or 'wet' chart. These subjects may enjoy carpentry, car maintenance and so on. They may move house fairly frequently and they may make money out of property. They can be quarrelsome in the home or they may simply shout rather ineffectually at their spouses and children. They may 'whine' about supposed problems or about their health. This placement is a surprisingly sexy one because there is a need to connect with the loved one on the deepest level. The breasts, lungs and stomachs are sensitive.

Fifth   These subjects are usually strong and robust. They are keen on sports and games and may be very competitive. They make excellent salesmen and women. They can be pushy parents who want their children to compete and to win. They are good with children and young people and they may work or spend their spare time with them. This is supposed to be a very sexy placement, but sometimes the sex drive can be channelled into work or creativity rather than lovemaking. The back and heart are weak spots.

Sixth   These subjects can work very hard when their interest is aroused but they can switch off and simply serve time if their jobs don't hold their interest. Some are hard on subordinates, using their considerable communications skills to cutting effect, while others with this placement are very kind and thoughtful to other people. These people make good critics and they can use their critical skills to hurt or to amuse. Some of them talk incessantly, others are 'nit-pickers' but, to be honest, they bring more pain to themselves than they do to others. Some of these subjects use sex in order to get what they want out of life while others are excellent lovers who enjoy giving and receiving sexual pleasure. The skin, bowels and intestines may be sensitive.

Seventh　An energetic attitude to marriage and partnerships. Can be quarrelsome and the cause of their own disappointments in relationships. Some people with this placement wait for others to validate them because they have no clear idea of their own worth. Sex is always an issue with this placement and it may be the best part of these subjects' lives, although it can, in some instances, be engaged in purely to keep a partner happy or pushed aside altogether for the sake of some other aim. The kidneys, bladder and other internal organs can be weak.

Eighth　Attracted to the medical profession, especially surgery. Butchery is another possible career as are mining, engineering, the armed forces or weaponry. Can be keen on detection and investigation, forensic or insurance matters. There may be a deep interest in death or the afterlife. These subjects can be sexy, jealous and possibly conscience-ridden over their sexual pursuits. They can have difficulties in partnerships due to sexual matters. They may have health problems relating to the reproductive organs or the lower back. The throat can be sensitive too.

Ninth　These subjects are more active than intellectual. They make good sportspeople or adventurers, being interested in travel, often to unknown regions. Some of these subjects are indefatigable chasers after members of the opposite sex, while others actively seek intellectual activity and may spend their lives studying. These people have a well-developed sense of fair play and they may be keen lawyers. They may choose to

work in the travel trade or the legal, educational,
literary or religious professions. Their hips and legs
may be weak spots.

Tenth   Can be hard, energetic workers who reach the top alone.
These subjects can be ruthlessly ambitious. They may
be attracted to politics, engineering or the armed forces.
Very big business enterprises attract them, as does
banking. Depending upon other factors on the chart,
these people can actually relax into a good family or
sexual relationship and can pour their considerable
energies into lovemaking. Others can concentrate their
energies so strongly on their ambitions that sex
becomes an unwanted or unneeded extra in their lives.
Their weak spots are the skin, ears, teeth, bones, knees
and shins.

Eleventh   Clubs and societies are liked and group work or group
activities of all kinds appeal. These subjects make
wonderfully enthusiastic friends but they can fall out
with others just as quickly as they fall in with them.
They are attracted to causes and may be interested in
politics. These subjects are somewhat mercurial where
sex is concerned, being very interested in it at some
stages of their lives and totally uninterested at others.
The ankles and circulation are the weak spots.

Twelfth   These subjects live a rich inner life and they will spend
some part of their lives on an inward or spiritual
journey. They may be self-sacrificial towards family or
friends. They care for the condition of others and see
themselves as part of the wider world, needing to put
something back into life rather than succeeding at the
expense of others. These people may be introverted and
shy. Some can spend their lives dreaming and achieving
nothing, but this may not matter because their prayers
and inward thoughts actually aid the world in a strange
and subtle way. In some cases, there is a considerable
amount of suppressed anger and there may be feelings
of love which have to be kept hidden. Their sexual

feelings may be denied, or they may simply have to spend some part of their lives without the solace of lovemaking. At other times, they may be able to wallow in their sexuality and explore it to the full. Their weak spots are their feet and legs, their circulation and, in some cases their lungs or body fluids.

Jupiter

First
Broad-minded and cheerful. These subjects may be lucky in life, either making money easily or attaching themselves to partners who become rich. Attracted to the Jupiterian pursuits of travel, education, publishing and broadcasting, religion or the law. They learn a great deal about whatever is represented by the sign which this planet occupies. For example, Jupiter in the first house in Scorpio could bring an interest in forensic or medical matters. Nice smile, friendly manner, happy-go-lucky outlook.

Second
Lucky with money and possessions. These subjects could make money easily but they may be too generous or open-handed to keep it. They can earn money by dealing with foreigners or foreign goods. Landowning, farming, animal husbandry or some other form of outdoor life can feature in these folks' lives.

Third
These subjects get on well with their brothers and sisters. They are quite studious and may do well academically either at school or later in life. They have a deep interest in communications and they may write or communicate for a living. Travel and foreigners are liked and these can play a large part in these people's lives.

Fourth
Good relationships with parents and a good home life characterise this placement. May move house often or may make money out of property matters. Some inherit property while others win a share in property through the courts. They can lack perspective or be too closely

focused on home or family matters. Some work from their homes in some way.

Fifth   All forms of speculation are lucky for these subjects and they are good at sports and the creative arts. They may make money from sports, art or some kind of glamour business. They may enjoy working with children or teaching them. They are religious or spiritual and they may teach in a Sunday school. These subjects may have a dramatic, larger-than-life manner and they may be restless and easily bored. Their children do well and can have lucky lives in their turn.

Sixth   These subjects are happy at work and they enjoy what they do. They make money from working and they could inherit a business. They may work in any of the Jupiterian professions, such as travel, the law, education and religion. Travel interests them and they are fond of animals. Hips and thighs may be weak or may suffer from accidents if other factors on the chart point to this.

Seventh   This is an excellent placement for partnerships both of the working and the personal kind. Marriage may be either very good or very bad. These subjects are friendly and flirtatious and they are especially attracted to foreigners or anyone who is different in some way. Pleasant and patient personalities.

Eighth   There is a strong chance that these subjects could inherit money. There may be a particularly easy or casual attitude towards death and the afterlife. These subjects may do very well from marriage and they could be attracted to partners from other countries or who are different in some way.

Ninth   All the Jupiterian interests are heightened with this placement which means that these subjects may travel a lot or be interested in religious or spiritual matters. They may teach or work in the law, publishing or the media. These people are happy, lucky and sometimes reckless. They can be outspoken, eccentric or tactless. Their hips and thighs may be weak.

Tenth   These subjects do well in their chosen career and may achieve public acclaim. They have a good manner in business or politics and can be successful without making a great deal of effort. They usually make good money too. These people may have a rather dramatic and 'stagy' personality and they may need a good deal of variety in their working lives. They want to leave the world a better or a happier place than when they found it.

Eleventh These subjects have many friends and acquaintances, some of them being rich and/or influential. They may have a strangely casual or a pompously high-minded attitude to others. They may embrace causes and they may use their wealth philanthropically.

Twelfth   These people prefer to work alone and they may achieve success in something like poetry, art or dancing. They like the sea and are keen on travel. These subjects are also interested in medicine, especially the alternative variety. They are talented and musical but gentle and shy when they are not on show or performing.

Saturn

First   These subjects' parents may have had difficulty in conceiving them or giving birth. They may be conscious of having lived before and of not wanting to come back on this occasion! These people are inhibited, shy and rather serious but this may be covered up by an act of some kind. They take work and life seriously and they take a responsible attitude to all that they do. They may be ailing as children and/or suffer from chronic ailments in adulthood. Tinnitus, psoriasis or bone problems are typical. They are often happier in old age and their tendency to work hard pays off by giving them tremendous success and a very high income later in life. Strangely enough, Saturn on the ascendant, or any other hard Saturn aspect can lead to fame and fortune!

Second   These subjects work hard to make money and they succeed in due course. Success is hard-won but almost inevitable. They can be possessive and stingy.

Third   A hard early life with problems at school. Success and self-education come later through these subjects' own efforts. They help their brothers and sisters and have formal but good relations with their neighbours.

Fourth   An unhappy and deprived early life. Could have restrictive parents who may have been stingy and cruel. These subjects work hard to obtain a good family and home of their own and they value these things when they have them. Their early problems may not have been due to bad parenting but to poverty or tribulation in the family.

Fifth   These subjects may have a domineering parent (usually the father). They may lack joy, or they may work too hard and forget how to play. Alternatively, they may take a serious attitude to creative endeavours and make a great success out of these. Children may be seen as a burden but, alternatively, they can be much loved and very successful in their turn. Some people with this placement choose not to have children or they may have difficulty in producing children.

Sixth   These subjects are hard workers with a serious attitude to their jobs but they may not enjoy the work that they do. They may suffer from backaches. Although this house is not concerned with children, I have found that Saturn placed here can bring difficulties in either having children or bringing them up.

Seventh   These people may marry late and to someone who is much older or much younger than themselves. There may be restriction or frustration in marriage or as a result of marriage or business partnerships. They are faithful partners with a serious attitude to the partnership.

Eighth   A careful, responsible attitude to money, especially when dealing with other people's resources. Can have sexual problems, or be morbid and miserable. On the other hand, all these areas of life may work out well once the subject gets into middle age.

Ninth Deep thinkers who are dedicated to causes which benefit mankind. These subjects are happier when they get older. Long-distance travel and foreigners may bring them trouble but, alternatively, these may bring increased status or money. These subjects may spend a lifetime searching for spiritual experiences or some kind of meaning to their lives.

Tenth Could be ambitious to the exclusion of social and family life. Obligations can weigh heavily. These subjects may be efficient and conscientious at work but they may never enjoy their work. They may switch career in mid-life and achieve a great deal of success later on. They may achieve fame and fortune and/or suffer public disgrace.

Eleventh These subjects may take committees and group activities very seriously. They may have influential friends whom they use in order to get on. Alternatively, they may be too busy with their jobs to have any friends. Elderly relatives and friends may help them to get on in life.

Twelfth This placement can lead to sadness and also to mental problems or an inability to express thoughts. These people may find themselves married to a partner who doesn't talk or listen to them. They may feel lonely although surrounded by family. They may be their own worst enemy. Some turn early suffering, an ailing childhood or their own super-sensitivity to suffering to advantage by becoming nurses, counsellors, astrologers or carers. These subjects learn to discipline their inner selves and may learn to cope by using meditative techniques.

Uranus

First Intelligent, unpredictable, individualistic. Should have a modern, scientific mind but may have unusual ideas or an unusual lifestyle. May have nerve or circulation problems. Friends could be extremely important to these subjects.

Second   Unpredictable income. These subjects may have gains and losses on a grand scale. They may have two or more different sources of income. Sudden loss or gains of job or an unusual way of gaining possessions, resources. Non-materialist attitude to life. Friends may help these subjects to find something that they value in life, but their values would be unusual in any case.

Third   Frequent changes of school and/or an unusual education. Lively, intelligent mind with unusual ideas. Odd experiences or an odd attitude to brothers and sisters. May become close to friends and treat them like brothers and sisters. Friends may educate these subjects.

Fourth   Unstable situation early in life with many upheavals or changes of home. Could have been disruptive and odd when a child. May choose to live in an unusual home or under strange circumstances later in life. May choose to make a home with a friend.

Fifth   May chase after strange love affairs or peculiar sexual experiences. Lively, intelligent mind, possibly an inventor, certainly creative in an unusual way. Could have unusual pastimes or hobbies. Will have clever children. Could be inspired by friends and could have casual love affairs with friends who become lovers and then slip back to being friends once again.

Sixth   Can be unpredictable at work. May have two jobs or one very unusual one. May have sudden illnesses such as circulation problems or paralysis. May have many friends at or through work.

Seventh   An unusual and very free marriage is needed. Must have mental rapport with any partner. Could choose unusual people for partners. Working partnerships could be very odd. Could choose to live with a friend and have sexual relationships away from the home.

Eighth   Unusual ideas in the realm of work, money and sex.

Could gain and lose money from business partnerships or marriage circumstances. May inherit. May be morbid or obsessed by sex. May be attached to a strange or obsessive partner. May have an unusual attitude to friends.

Ninth   Could spend a lot of time travelling and have great gains and losses as a result. Could be a very lucky gambler. Accident-prone and also prone to mental stress. Could be an excellent clairvoyant or medium. May be keen on helping groups of people to understand religion, spirituality, etc. Could make friends through hobbies, interests or while travelling.

Tenth   Possible sudden changes in career, because these subjects dislike routine. Far-sighted with leadership qualities. May have two jobs which are equally important to each other but very different from one another. May make good friends at work or choose to work with groups of friends. May work with or for groups of people. Keen on education in order to get on in life. May work as astrologers.

Eleventh These subjects like societies, clubs and group activities. They have many friends but they gain and lose them quickly. These people might be eccentric or different in some way. May be keen astrologers. Far-sighted, broad-minded, these people never stop educating themselves.

Twelfth   These subjects may have terrific clairvoyant abilities and they may be keen on astrology. Secretive, they may harbour odd ideas and feelings. Could be very spiritual and mystical. These people may hide their emotions or they may be confused by them or be upset by feelings of inner turmoil. Eccentric.

Neptune

First   These subjects are dreamy, sensitive and artistic. They may be impractical, disorganised, chaotic and forgetful. Some are eccentric, whereas others may be fairly normal but drawn to mystical or artistic pursuits. They are often talented, musical or artistic and some make excellent photographers.

Second May not be able to keep money for long or possibly mean and money-minded. Usually non-materialistic in outlook. These subjects value kindness and caring for others. They may make money from mystical or other unusual interests. They may work successfully in something to do with liquids such as the oil industry, sailing, fishing, shipping, plumbing, etc. They like aesthetic or artistic objects.

Third These subjects are intuitive and imaginative. They may lack concentration or they may have a wonderful gift of communication through visual effects (video, photography) or through descriptive writing. Could be some kind of therapist. Good actor, but may be something of a drifter.

Fourth These subjects may love their homes but they may not keep them very tidy. Alternatively, the home could be a spotless thing of great beauty. There should be a good relationship with the parents with an intuitive, telepathic link. May be disorganised in practical matters but with a strong imagination or inner life.

Fifth Very creative and imaginative. Could have a career on the stage or something similar. These subjects tend to be escapist at times, they may prefer television and books to real life or they may simply have a strong inner life. Fond of dancing and of the sea. May love wild countryside and trees in particular. Should have excellent rapport with small children and a good, if odd, relationship with their own children.

Sixth Can be very creative and may work hard on their chosen projects, but otherwise, they can be lazy and uninterested in work. Interested in humanitarian causes or working in an artistic or mystical sphere. May work as a nurse or with the mentally-handicapped or a similar kind of occupation. Allergic to drugs and such things as seafood or monosodium glutamate. May be drawn to work on or near water or with liquids (cooking, hairdressing).

Seventh   These subjects either have wonderfully happy marriages or confused and difficult ones. They may be very independent or they may lean heavily on their partners. They may have vague attitudes to life or they may be quite sensible but with a tendency to draw drunken or chaotic people to them. They may have an idealised vision of relationships. They would be taken for a ride in any kind of business or working partnership.

Eighth   Could be very psychic and drawn to the world of mysticism, the occult or to spiritualism. Very intuitive and mediumistic, more in touch with the other side than here for much of the time. Could squander inheritance or a partner's money or alternatively, they could be 'taken for a ride' by a partner. They may choose an artistic partner and/or enjoy an absolutely ideal relationship where sex is elevated to a spiritual level. They may have strange love affairs with peculiar people.

Ninth   Could work in the field of philosophy or religion. May be inspired. May do well in trades connected to the sea or to liquids, such as the oil industry, hairdressing, etc. Could travel a great deal and could fall in love while travelling. May be involved in strange legal cases which go on for years. These subjects help people who are in trouble or who cannot help themselves.

Tenth   These subjects may choose a career for idealistic reasons. They may work in feminine or creative fields such as photography, art, dancing, poetry or something similar. Alternatively, they could choose nursing, working with prisoners, the mentally-handicapped, or in some other form of caring occupation. They aspire to something greater than simply earning money and they want to heal the world. Some work with liquids such as oil, the sea or the 'booze' industry. They may go through many changes in life and they could be greatly helped or let down by others in career matters. May start off well and then let everything come to naught.

Eleventh   Idealistic, artistic and creative, these subjects may find it hard to get anything done at all. Their aims are intellectual and artistic and they are keen on groups who have the same kind of goal. Could be greatly helped or badly let down by friends. May be mystical, intuitive and interested in astrology.

Twelfth   Likely to be interested in poetry, ballet, culture, art and music. Could be a great animal lover or a lover of people, especially those who need help. Mystical, spiritual and other-worldly. May have great sadness in life or simply be drawn inwards to a contemplative existence.

Pluto

First   These subjects have attractive, magnetic personalities and dynamic natures. They are attracted to big business or to positions of power and authority. Their lives go in distinct phases with gains and losses every few years. Can brood and have a terrible temper. They tend to control or rule others if they can.

Second   Can make very big money but may lose it on a grand scale too. These subjects have a good grasp of business affairs. They also have a deep need for security, and may see money and possessions as a form of this. They can be covetous or they may be hoarders.

Third   These subjects have terrific powers of concentration and they finish the projects that they start. They can be moody and depressed at times. They may do much to help their siblings or, alternatively, they can be beastly to them. These people can make money by teaching and writing and they enjoy influencing others via the medium of words.

Fourth   These people feel very deeply about their homes, their parents and their marriage partners. They may try to control or dominate their families and they may be too fond of their own point of view when in the home situation. They may inherit property.

Fifth   Children are important to these subjects and they may go to a lot of trouble, either to have children or to bring them up. They may live for pleasure or, alternatively they may take a serious view of pastimes, sports and so on. These people enjoy the arts and music, and they could be drawn to gambling in order to make money. Some have many affairs, others put their energies into creative schemes.

Sixth   May be a very hard worker or may simply be too concerned with working life. These people try to reform or change their colleagues' working practices. They may have weak health or irritable bowels and some of these problems may be due to tension.

Seventh   Could be very good business partners but possibly a bit overbearing. Could be very demanding marriage partners with too much emphasis on sex. Feelings are intense and jealousy is a problem, but these subjects may be on the receiving end of this kind of treatment rather than dishing it out themselves. May inherit from a partner.

Eighth   Very intuitive, especially where money and business is concerned. May inherit from a partner. May work for the community or in a mediumistic or spiritual manner. Could be very keen on Plutonic interests such as the afterlife, death, sex, birth, medical or forensic and investigative matters. Could deal with the insides or the underneath of things, e.g. butchery, mining or simply digging out secrets. Very secretive themselves. Analytical, logical, with very searching minds. Could be great animal lovers.

Ninth   Very spiritual. These people may be bound up with foreigners or distant places. They may force their religious or spiritual views on others, or they may drag others through the courts. Could be very keen on educating themselves and others. Could be very fond of animals, or keen to travel to strange places.

Tenth   These subjects can reach great heights of influence or they can attach themselves to influential people. They may work in fields where they can influence others or even take them over in some way. For instance, this is a good placement for hypnotherapists, anaesthetists and dream analysts. There may be powerful urges to rule and these subjects may be obsessed with dreams of grandeur. May be attracted to drugs or may work with them. Dynamic, powerful or completely crazy person.

Eleventh   These people may be looking for the truth and may choose astrology as a method for doing this. These subjects may have powerful and influential friends or, alternatively, they may try to influence groups of people or to make friends of people in order to change or influence them. Generally speaking, they are friendly, likeable and fond of working for committees, clubs and societies. They are likely to be well-balanced and sensible, although with one or two funny ideas from time to time.

Twelfth   These subjects have hidden talents and interests. They may go in for hidden or taboo love affairs of some sort. They may have hidden problems of a psychological kind, such as suppressed anger or hatred for something that has been done to them by others. They may strive to find some kind of mystical or astrological truth and then express this to others in the form of poetry or music.

CHAPTER 10

Aspects

This is a very tricky area of astrology for a beginner to get to grips with. The first problem is that it is natural to think of aspects in terms of *good* and *bad*, but that is really too black and white to be applied in such a way. Astrology books use such terms as *easy*, *beneficial* and *good* as well as *challenging*, *difficult*, *tense* or *stressful* to describe aspects and this can be confusing. Worse still, they often use the terms *hard* and *soft* to describe aspects, and this is even more confusing because these terms don't mean what they sound like at all! Let me try to make things clear for you.

Hard and Soft Aspects

The term 'hard aspect' does not refer to the nature of the aspect, it is not automatically *bad* or *difficult*. This is a geometric term which simply means that a planet is in conjunction, square or opposition to another planet or to an angle such as the ascendant, descendant, midheaven or the nadir. These are the kinds of aspects that we are most likely to become aware of during the course of our lives. All the other aspects are called *soft* aspects. Some of these, such as the sextile and trine are pleasant but others, such as the inconjunct and semi-square can be quite awkward, so once again the terms refer to the geometrical type of aspect rather than the way it affects a subject. Other terms such as beneficial, stressful, etc. mean what you think they mean, that is good and kindly or bad and unpleasant.

Good and Bad Aspects

Good, *benefical*, *easy* or any other behavioural term that may be applied to an aspect is always relative because this depends upon so many factors. For instance, a trine between Venus and Neptune in the second and sixth houses in Leo and Sagittarius could bring pots of money, travel and world-wide fame through creative exploits. A trine between Saturn and Uranus anywhere on the chart could simply make these planets less of a pain in the neck than usual! *Bad*, *challenging* or *difficult* aspects can be the building blocks which enable us to succeed and/or they can be a terrible handicap. Often it is by overcoming our limitations and dealing with our handicaps that we actually manage to succeed, therefore a truly bad aspect can turn out to be a blessing in disguise. How many people have you heard say that they have done more, achieved more and become more due to having to overcome hurdles?

What are Allowable Orbs?

A conjunction occurs when two planets are in the same place. For example, Jupiter and Pluto both at 20 degrees of Cancer. However, these planets would still be in conjunction with each other if they were anything up to eight degrees apart, such as Jupiter at 16 degrees of Cancer and Pluto at 24 degrees of Cancer. This would be called a wide conjunction, whereas if they were both were at exactly the same degree and minute (both at 20 deg 11 minutes), it would be an exact conjunction. Exactly exact conjunctions or exactly exact aspects of any kind are extremely rare, so there is usually a bit of leeway. Astrologers disagree about the 'allowability' of the orbs, thus, if you are told by another astrologer that the orb of a square should be as much as ten degrees or as little as six degrees, don't let this worry you. Just use whatever orb you feel is comfortable.

----------------Table of Aspects----------------

Symbol	Name	Distance Between Planets or Angles	Allowable Orb
☌	Conjunction	0°	8°
☍	Opposition	180°	8°
△	Trine	120°	8°
□	Square	90°	8°
✳	Sextile	60°	6°
∠	Semi-square	45°	2°
⚼	Sesquiquadrate	135°	2°
⚻	Inconjunct or Quincunx	150°	2°
⚺	Semi-sextile	30°	2°
Q	Quintile	72°	2°
BQ	Bi-quintile	144°	2°

--------------Moving the Goal Posts--------------

The following story comes directly from my heart! When I was a youngster, I tried my hand at learning maths because I am attracted to the precision and logic of the subject. I found that the authors of maths books would demonstrate a particular problem and then provide a series of exercises for the student to work out. Invariably, there would be one (maybe even two) which was very much like the example, but all the rest would be totally different and therefore, to me, completely incomprehensible! These books seemed to assume knowledge that I, for one, certainly did not have, plus the ability to make a quantum leap from one idea to another, totally disassociated, one! Maths teachers weren't much help either because they were invariably as inarticulate as the text books they used, and they always moved on to a new topic before I was completely confident in my ability to handle the previous one.

I eventually came to the conclusion that a) most people would be quite good at maths if the books stuck to exercises which matched up with the examples, and b) if the teachers actually allowed students time to absorb a new concept and also made a point of building the students' confidence. I have also long since decided that c) all successful mathematics students are people who have done it in a previous life and therefore, only need a bit of a refresher course in this one.

The point of this sad diatribe is to explain that, in true maths-book-writer form, I am happy to tell you that now you have got a good grasp of the rules of the aspects, you must now know the exceptions to these rules!

The Exceptions

Any aspect to the nodes of the Moon should be pretty much exact. You could allow yourself an orb of a couple of degrees perhaps, for a hard aspect (conjunction, square or opposition) and only one degree of orb for anything else. Much the same would go for Chiron. In the case of the astrological oddments, such as the part of fortune, vertex, east point or the other asteroids, only one degree of orb should be allowed.

Back to the Rules Once More:
The Conjunction

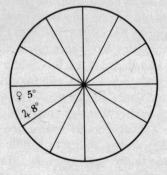

Conjunction

As you can see from the table on page 169 and this diagram, a conjunction occurs when two planets are within eight degrees of each other. This – as you are quite aware by now – is a 'hard' aspect. This brings the force of two planets (or a planet and an angle) to bear down hard on one area of the chart. A conjunction may involve more than two planets but, obviously, only one angle, at once. This is a strong, forceful and very important aspect and it can be good, bad or a mixture of both, depending on various factors.

Example 1: a conjunction between Mercury and Venus is a nice thing to have because it enhances a subject's ability to communicate pleasantly and the sign and house which are showcased would show how this communications ability could best be utilised.

Example 2: a conjunction between Venus and Saturn may inhibit a subject's ability to relate well to others. Such a conjunction may bring poor health, a shortage of money or a variety of other ills depending upon the sign and house that the conjunction occurs in.

——————— The Opposition ———————

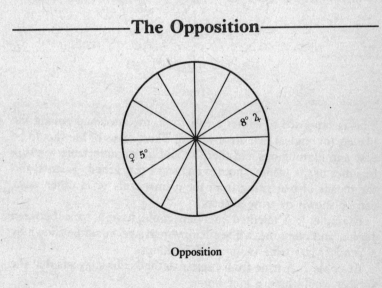

Opposition

This is a tense aspect which brings the two signs and houses concerned into focus. The aspect sets up challenges and, therefore, is often found in the charts of successful people. Remember, the so-called *bad* aspects are often the building blocks of success.

Example: an opposition between malefic planets (to use a very old-fashioned term), such as Saturn and Mars, between the sixth and twelfth houses will bring an emphasis on health matters. The subject may have to cope with a chronic problem within his own body (sixth) or he may make sacrifices due to the bad health of others (twelfth).

The Trine

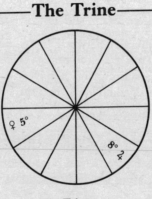

Trine

This is supposed to confer creativity in the areas and among the planets (or angles) that are involved. These areas of life should be easy and harmonious and there should be a comfortable working together of the planets, houses and signs concerned. Talents, and the means of benefiting from them financially or in other ways, can be shown by trine aspects.

Example 1: a talented medium could have a trine between Jupiter and Neptune, while a happy marriage would be shown by a Venus/Mars trine (among other things).

Example 2: A trine from Jupiter to the Nadir suggests that the subject would have a nice home.

The Square

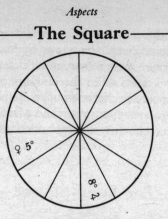

Square

This represents an awkward situation in any chart but, like the opposition, squares are commonly found in the charts of successful people because the subjects have to work hard to overcome the problems which the squares set up for them.

Example 1: a Sun/Mars square could bring success in adventurous or dangerous sports or occupations. The root of this could be that the subject has a sneaking feeling that, when the chips are down, he would act like a coward. He may, therefore, set out to put himself in dangerous situations and generally behave like Rambo in order to prove to himself that this is not true.

Example 2: a Saturn/Ascendant square would bring career struggles.

The Sextile

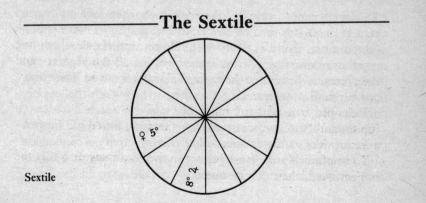

Sextile

This is similar to the trine in that it should be beneficial in its effects and it shows where talents can be used. However, the effects of this are more mental than physical and would probably manifest themselves as an ability to communicate or, possibly, to make some kind of commercial use out of the planets concerned.

Example: Venus sextile Jupiter would confer a pleasant manner and it could bring benefits through relationships or working partnerships.

The Semi-Square

Semi-Square

This is supposed to be a slightly difficult aspect but as always, take note of the planets, angles, signs and houses that are involved. Being a 45 degree aspect, this is difficult to spot when looking over a chart. Perhaps it is for this reason, in addition to its relative lack of importance, that it is rarely used. However, there shouldn't be any excuse nowadays because computers list all the aspects and it only remains to glance at the signs and houses involved. Therefore, find your semi-squares and consider them to be vaguely challenging, difficult, bad, stressful and otherwise not very nice.

Example: a semi-square between Venus and Pluto could suggest minor forms of manipulation and underhand activity in connection with a relationship. If houses that concerned money or business were involved, then this is where the problem would lie.

──────The Sesquiquadrate──────

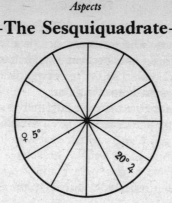

Sesquiquadrate

I should imagine that most astrologers would have great difficulty in pronouncing these, let alone interpreting them! A sesquiquadrate is supposed to be vaguely unpleasant but less so than the semi-square. Having said that, I was quite frighteningly ill recently and the only aspects which occurred by transit on that day were two simultaneous sesquiquadrates to my Sun from different planets in different areas of my chart.

Example: a sesquiquadrate between Jupiter and Mars might mean that one has to work or live among men (Mars = men) who have little time for a subject's beliefs or who seek to restrict him in some vague kind of way. This is not likely to be a major problem, however.

──────The Inconjunct (or Quincunx)──────

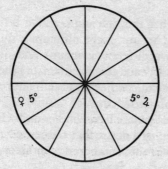

Inconjunct

This is a really awkward aspect which can bring confusion and tension to any chart. The worst scenario is a 'yod' aspect which involves a double inconjunct between two planets which are sextile to each other and both 150 degrees away from another which opposes the mid-point between them.

Example: any inconjunct can be extremely irritating, and these 'nasties' seem to be particularly fond of attaching themselves to the signs, houses and planets which deal with love, marriage and personal relationships of all kinds. The subject needs to develop real awareness of his or her nature and the kind of behaviour patterns which keep repeatedly throwing him/her back into the same pit.

The Semi-Sextile

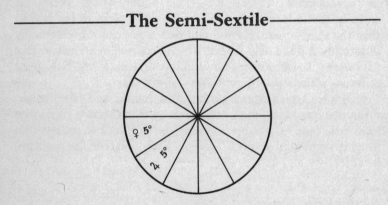

Semi-Sextile

Some astrologers like this one and consider it to be vaguely lucky but I think it can set up slight difficulties due to the fact that adjacent signs have different elements and qualities from each other. Mercury and Venus are never far from the Sun or from each other, therefore semi-sextiles between one or other of these planets is quite common.

Example: A semi-sextile between Venus in Gemini and the Sun in Cancer would bring a desire for security, a settled home life and a family gathered around one. Venus in Gemini would long for freedom (especially in a woman's chart) and would try to side-step any form of 'entrapment'. On a man's chart, he could want family life but he would be attracted to intellectual, freedom-loving women. To be honest, a semi-sextile is not a big deal and any problems that it does set up are not that hard to solve.

Quintile and Bi-Quintile

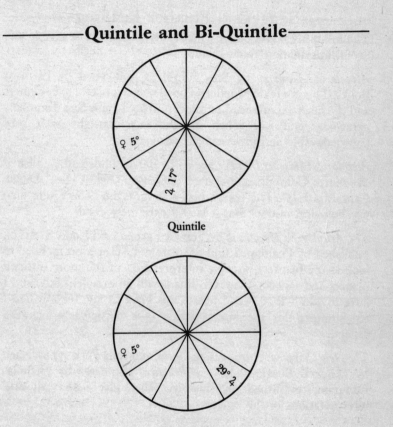

Quintile

Bi-Quintile

Both are supposed to confer talent or skills. These talents would be attached to the planets and houses that are involved.

Example: a Quintile between Mars in Taurus and Pluto in Leo

would give a subject the ability to put his talents to work and to finish whatever he started. If these were also Mars in the twelfth house and Pluto in the third, he may be able to write books on occult subjects. (Guess who has just such a Quintile)?

──────── Suggested Further Reading ────────

The following books either concentrate on aspects or give lots of useful information about them.

Aspects in Astrology by Sue Tompkins, published by Element Books. This is a really wonderful book which is useful to beginners and the most experienced astrologers alike. I know Sue Tompkins personally and can vouch for the fact that she is a very knowledgeable and experienced astrologer.

Astrological Insights Into Personality by Betty Lundstead, published by Astro Computing Services, PO Box 16430, San Diego, California 92116. This book is biased towards the 1970s Californian psychological outlook but it is still extremely good.

The Astrologer's Handbook by Francis Sakoian and Louis S. Acker, published by Penguin. I find Sakoian and Acker a bit inclined to look at the blackest possible interpretation of the more difficult planets and aspects. However, this is still an excellent buy, and I have to admit that I tend to use this book as my 'bible' when I am stumped for the interpretation of a particularly awkward aspect.

The New Compleat Astrologer by Derek and Julia Parker, published by Mitchell Beazley and *The Practical Astrologer* by Nicholas Campion, published by Hamlyn also give good 'quickie' interpretations of the aspects.

APPENDIX 1
Astrology and Health

I am tackling this aspect of astrology as a separate section because it is not particularly straightfoward. The theory is that the body is divided up into twelve areas which are ruled by the twelve signs of the zodiac and also by their ruling planets. However, there is a lot more to astrological diagnosis than this and there are a number of people who specialise in this area. These people are often alternative healers, herbalists, and so on. If you are really interested in this aspect of astrology, you must find such a person to instruct you.

In my own experience, I have found that the position of the Sun, the ascendant and especially the Moon, all have something to say about the health of a client, in addition to specific signs, houses and planets which may be affected. Often a combination of planets and aspects indicates a health problem. Planets in the sixth house are not necessarily an indication of poor health, and even transits or progressions to the sixth are not always health-orientated. A severe affliction of a planet in the sixth would be a good indicator of a health problem but so can much else that is on a birthchart. This is a very tricky area of astrology and it needs a lot of practice before plunging in with both feet. Until you are sure that you know what you are doing, I should avoid frightening clients by trying to give them too much health information!

The following list and diagram show the basic relationship between signs, planets and parts of the body.

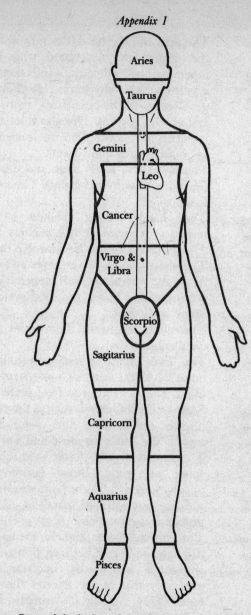

Parts of the body and astrological correspondences

Aries/Mars	The eyes and the head, down to just below the upper jaw. Associated with sudden inflammatory ailments, infections and accidents, especially burns. Headaches and problems with the circulatory, reproductive and urinary systems. This also rules acts and incidents of violence. Also eye problems such as conjunctivitis and squints.
Taurus/Venus	The lower jaw, lower teeth and the throat, (including the thyroid gland). The neck and lower spine.
Gemini/Mercury	The hands, arms, shoulders, upper respiratory tract and the nervous system. Also rules the mind. Can involve the skin.
Cancer/Moon	The chest, thorax, lower lungs and breasts. Also the stomach and upper digestive system, eating habits and food preferences. Some body fluids.
Leo/Sun	The spine, the heart, the arteries and the circulation.
Virgo/Mercury	The lower digestive system, intestines and bowels. Also the skin, nervous system and the mind. Eating habits and food preferences.
Libra/Venus	Some of the soft organs such as the pancreas, bladder and kidneys. Also motor development – the ability to move and walk.
Scorpio/Pluto and Mars	The sexual organs, lower stomach, lower spine and groin. Blood disorders. The unconscious and unusual situations such as sudden, unexplained paralysis. Also eye problems, squints, etc.
Sagittarius/Jupiter	The hips and thighs, and also the circulation through the legs. The liver, pituitary gland and some parts of the circulatory system, especially that of the arteries through the legs. (My medically-trained husband suggested that I mention the femoral artery

which is inside the thighs.)

Capricorn/Saturn The knees, but also the skin, bones, ears and teeth. Also the gall bladder, the vagus nerves and the spleen. Associated with chronic ailments, especially rheumatism and diseases of old age. Also breathing, asthma and eczema.

Aquarius/Uranus and Saturn The ankles and the circulation to the extremities. Also breathing. This is also associated with nervous breakdowns and cramp.

Pisces/Neptune The feet, the lungs and some body fluids. Allergic conditions and ailments caused by misuse of drink or drugs. Nervous debility, confusion, and peculiar mental states.

The Four Humours

While writing this section, I stopped to chat to Jonathan Dee and he supplied the following information from a medieval book on the four humours.

Fire people
Nature: Hotness (the spelling is medieval)
Quality: Hot/dry
Organ: Spleen
Humour: Choleric
Temperament: Bilious
Character: Excitable
Ailments: Jaundice, cholera

Earth people
Nature: Dryness
Quality: Cold/dry
Organ: Spleen

Humour:	Black bile
Temperament:	Melancholic
Character:	Brooding, suspicious
Ailments:	Cancer, paralysis, epilepsy

Air people

Nature:	Wetness
Quality:	Hot/wet
Organ:	Liver
Humour:	Blood
Temperament:	Sanguine
Character:	Optimistic, lively, impulsive
Ailments:	Apoplexy, neuraesthenia

Water people

Nature:	Coldness
Quality:	Cold/wet
Organ:	Lungs, brain
Humour:	Phlegm
Temperament:	Phlegmatic
Character:	Cold, tranquil, sluggish
Ailments:	Rheumatism, colds and worms

This following key may throw even more confusion on the whole business:

Element	*Colour*	*Taste*	*Planet*	*Season*
Fire:	Red	Bitter	Mars	Summer
Earth:	Green	Sour	Saturn	Winter
Air:	Yellow	Salt	Venus	Spring
Water:	Blue	Sweet	Jupiter	Autumn

There were plenty of subdivisions of these elements and planets with hot/wet/dry/cold bits here and there and it was by this means that the old sages made their diagnoses. A cold/wet ailment would have been treated by something hot and dry which came under the rulership of Mars; for example, wetted mustard powder. Mustard footbaths for colds were around until about a hundred years ago. I should think that a mustard plaster would be quite helpful for rheumatic inflammation even now, so perhaps there was something in it. It seems to me that this kind of thinking is not very different from that of traditional Oriental medicine. The Asians and Orientals look at the elements which rule *both* the patient and the disease and they treat both accordingly.

APPENDIX 2

Astrology and Colours

Those of you who have an artistic bent may wish to draw your birthcharts by hand, using the appropriate colours for specific Sun signs or planets. Just for you, here is a list supplied by my 'astrologically-correct' friend, Jonathan Dee, of the right colours to choose from:

The Signs

The fire signs (Aries, Leo, Sagittarius)	Red
The earth signs (Taurus, Virgo, Capricorn)	Brown
The air signs (Gemini, Libra, Aquarius)	Palest blue
The water signs (Cancer, Scorpio, Pisces)	Dark blue

The Planets

The Sun	Gold, orange, orangey-yellow
The Moon	Silver, white
Mercury	Yellow, black and white check (yes, really!)
Venus	Green, pink
Mars	Bright red
Jupiter	Royal blue, imperial purple
Saturn	Black
Uranus	Neon or dayglo colours, bright purple, ultra-violet
Neptune	Swirly blues and greens, sea colours with silver fishy colours mixed in amongst them
Pluto	Infra-red, dark red, dark purple

APPENDIX 3

Astrology and Tarot

In conclusion, I thought it would be interesting to look at something completely different. I have never tried to link the Tarot to astrology because I have always considered it best to use each method of divination quite separately, as each one relies upon its own strengths (and weaknesses). However, as an experiment I decided to play around with the major Arcana and see if it fitted the energies of the planets, and I found that all the cards matched at least one planet, while some of them matched more than one.

Astrology	*Tarot*
The Sun	The Sun, The Magician, The Emperor
The Moon	The Moon, The High Priestess
Mercury	The Magician, The Chariot, Temperance
Venus	The Empress, The Lovers, Temperance
Mars	The Emperor, The Chariot
Jupiter	The Hierophant, Justice, The Chariot
Saturn	The Hermit, The Hanged Man, Strength
Uranus	The Star, The Tower
Neptune	The Moon, The Hanged Man
Pluto	The Devil, Death, The World, Judgement
The Zodiac	The Wheel of Fortune

APPENDIX 4
The Last Word

It is hard to know just what to put in and what to leave out of a book like this, because astrology is such a large and fascinating subject. I haven't gone into the aspects between the planets and angles in detail because that would have made this book too large. There are a number of excellent works on the market which specialise in this facet of astrology but, who knows, I may decide to do one myself one of these days. I have left the whole subject of predictive astrology out of this book for the same reason.

I hope that this book helps you to clarify what the planets are all about and how to use them in a natal chart. I think it is both simple enough and also comprehensive enough to fulfil that function successfully. Astrology students enjoy my books and seem to find them extremely useful, so let us hope that this, the fourth book in the *Sun Signs, Moon Signs* and *Rising Signs* series is as worthwhile an enterprise as the others have turned out to be. I put my whole heart and soul into every one of these books and I think that you, my regular book-buyers, are aware of that. Good luck with your astrological studies, because *your* success is also *my* success.

SUN SIGNS
Discover yourself and others through astrology

Much has been written about astrology and, in particular, Sun signs. However, in this unique book Sasha Fenton turns her inimitable astrological skills to the subject, revealing once and for all exactly what you want to know about your Sun sign.

Sign by sign, the book fully explains the significance of each sign, including such details as the Elements and the Qualities of each sign. It dispels any confusions regarding cusps or Summertime, and compares well-known celebrities with yourself. It will leave you with vital knowledge about health, hobbies, shopping habits, possessions, work, sex and, most important of all, not what it is like to *be* a particular sign, but what it is like to *live* with one.

MOON SIGNS
Discover the hidden power
of your emotions

Almost everyone knows their Sun sign and what it says about their basic personality. Rising signs reveal even more about their personality. But what does our Moon sign, the sign that governs our emotions, tell us?

The position of the Moon in our birthchart affects our deepest requirements, our innermost needs. It governs our attitudes to food, our unconscious motivations, our habits and, of course, our relationships. Complete with a simple, easy-to-use ephemeris to find your own Moon sign, Sasha Fenton's acclaimed book will help you to reveal the hidden power of your emotions — she even shows how your garden can benefit from an understanding of phases of the Moon.

RISING SIGNS
Discover the truth about
your personality

The sign of the zodiac rising on the eastern horizon when you are born — your Rising sign — reveals details about your outer personality and how it masks what is underneath: your looks, actions and outward behaviour may all be determined by your Rising sign. And, being based on the actual *time* of birth, it is a far more personal indicator of character than the more general Sun sign.

Here Sasha Fenton shows how to find your Rising sign and explains how it applies to you. In addition, she examines decanates, the modifying 'thirds' of the zodiac signs, and their subsidiary effects on the horoscope.

UNDERSTANDING
ASTROLOGY
First steps in chart interpretation

Understanding Astrology provides a concise introduction to the ancient art of astrology, showing how it can be used to assess a person's character. Ingenious short-cuts and quick-clue summaries are given to help the beginner quickly grasp the basic ideas, and all aspects of astrology are covered, from elements, houses and hemispheres to planets and their influence.

Complete with diagrams, sample birth charts and a glossary of terms, this book serves as an ideal starting point for anyone taking their first steps in the fascinating study of astrology.

LIVING PALMISTRY
Modern hand analysis explained

Sasha Fenton and Malcolm Wright are both practising palmists with over 50 years of hand-reading experience between them. They bring to this book much that is new and revolutionary in palmistry, yet in all cases the ideas have been thoroughly researched and backed up by numerous readings.

In this fully revised and expanded edition of their seminal *The Living Hand*, authors Sasha Fenton and Malcolm Wright combine stunningly clear illustrations with easy, straightforward text to make a book whose simplicity of presentation makes it ideal for anyone wishing to learn palmistry from scratch or to update their techniques.

Contents include:

- truly lifelike illustrations bringing depth, vision and precise accuracy
- new concepts, such as energy rhythms and sibling lines
- an accurate method of timing events on the hand
- numerous practical examples and case histories

FORTUNE-TELLING
BY TEA LEAVES
A practical guide to the ancient
art of tasseography

It is thought that tasseography (reading tea leaves) began in ancient China. They used to read the inside of their handleless teacups and the pattern formed by the tea leaves came to have a divinatory significance.

Sasha Fenton, author of the best-selling *Fortune-Telling by Tarot Cards*, has written this long-awaited practical guide for anyone who wants to dip into the future. Fully illustrated, the book covers everything you need to know, from the symbolism of the tea leaves and the significance of the different parts of the cup, to how (in the age of the tea-bag) to brew a proper cup of tea!

Contents include:

- a brief history of tea leaf divination
- making intuitive / interpretive readings
- cup preparation rituals
- an A-Z of all tea leaf shapes
- actual readings with explanations

FORTUNE-TELLING
BY TAROT CARDS
A beginner's guide to understanding the future using Tarot cards

Nobody knows for certain where Tarot cards originally came from, but they seem to have emerged in their present form during the fourteenth century. Since then they have appeared in many guises but always with the same function — as a means of seeing into the future.

Sasha Fenton, a professional Tarot Reader for over ten years, has written this book to be used alongside the cards so that the beginner can quickly gain access to the secrets which are locked within them.

Illustrated throughout with the hauntingly beautiful *Prediction Tarot Deck*, this book provides the novice with an ideal introduction to this fascinating form of divination.

Contents include:

- the origins of the Tarot
- an introduction to the Major and Minor arcanas
- clear interpretations of the cards
- quick clues to the cards' meanings
- simple, complex, and special purpose readings

SUN SIGNS	1 85538 021 8	£4.99	☐
MOON SIGNS	0 85030 552 7	£5.99	☐
RISING SIGNS	0 85030 751 1	£4.99	☐
UNDERSTANDING ASTROLOGY	1 85538 065 X	£4.99	☐
LIVING PALMISTRY	0 85030 969 7	£5.99	☐
FORTUNE-TELLING BY TEA LEAVES	0 85030 657 4	£3.99	☐
FORTUNE-TELLING BY TAROT CARDS	0 85030 445 8	£4.99	☐
TAROT IN ACTION!	0 85030 525 X	£4.99	☐
SUPERTAROT	1 85538 017 X	£5.99	☐

All these books are available from your local bookseller or can be ordered direct from the publishers.

To order direct just tick the titles you want and fill in the form below:

Name: _____

Address: _____

_____

_____ Postcode: _____

Send to: Thorsons Mail Order, Dept 3, HarperCollins*Publishers*, Westerhill Road, Bishopbriggs, Glasgow G64 2QT.
Please enclose a cheque or postal order or your authority to debit your Visa/Access account —

Credit card no: _____
Expiry date: _____
Signature: _____

— up to the value of the cover price plus:
UK & BFPO: Add £1.00 for the first book and 25p for each additional book ordered.

Overseas orders including Eire: Please add £2.95 service charge. Books will be sent by surface mail but quotes for airmail despatches will be given on request.

24 HOUR TELEPHONE ORDERING SERVICE FOR ACCESS/VISA CARDHOLDERS — TEL: 041 772 2281.